ETHICAL AND
POLITICAL THINKING

ETHICAL AND
POLITICAL THINKING

BY

E. F. CARRITT

Emeritus Fellow of University College

GREENWOOD PRESS, PUBLISHERS
WESTPORT, CONNECTICUT

The Library of Congress has catalogued this publication as follows:

Library of Congress Cataloging in Publication Data

Carritt, Edgar Frederick, 1876–
  Ethical and political thinking.

  Reprint of the 1947 ed. published by Clarendon
Press, Oxford.
  1. Ethics. 2. Political ethics. I. Title.
BJ1011.C27 1973   170   73-3020
ISBN 0-8371-6826-0

> The written word cannot by itself give much help in argument nor adequately express the truth. What is clearer and more satisfactory is first the argument about justice and goodness and beauty that goes on in a man's own mind and secondly the argument successfully planted as its offspring in the souls of others.
>
> Summary of PLATO's *Phaedrus*, 276–8.

Originally published in 1947
by The Clarendon Press, Oxford

Reprinted with the permission
of Oxford University Press

First Greenwood Reprinting 1973

Library of Congress Catalogue Card Number 73-3020

ISBN 0-8371-6826-0

Printed in the United States of America

PREFACE

THE title I have chosen is intended to indicate that I would claim better qualifications for reporting the way in which intelligent peoples' minds work and progress upon these topics than for establishing any novel conclusions. I would not claim particularly wide reading in the subject, but I have probably had as good opportunities as any man for serious discussion with both novices and experts. For nearly fifty years, most of the time as an Oxford tutor, I have spent some twelve hours weekly each term in discussing moral, political, and aesthetic philosophy with pupils and with colleagues either singly or in very small groups. This gives in round numbers nearly 15,000 hours of opportunity for mass observation of *Ethical and Political Thinking*.

My special gratitude is to my old tutor and friend Professor Prichard and to the late Mr. H. B. Joseph for our many conversations. Three former pupils, Professor Raphael of Otago University, Mr. J. L. Evans, lecturer of Magdalen College, Oxford, and Mr. D. Rees of Merton, my assistant at Aberdeen University, have given me valuable criticism of this book. In reading, apart from the well-known classics on the subject, I think I owe most to Richard Price's *Review of the Principal Questions and Difficulties in Morals* (a title whose characteristic clumsiness has perhaps prevented deserved popularity, but which would well fit the present work) and to Dr. Rashdall's *The Theory of Good and Evil*.

E. F. C.

1947

ERRATA

p. 83, last line
for should do *read* should have done

pp. 84–5
Note 1 on p. 84 and Note 2 on p. 85
should be transposed

p. 141, Note line 2
for chapter *read* book

ANALYSIS

PART I

ETHICAL THINKING

I. AIMS AND METHODS OF MORAL PHILOSOPHY

II. THE GROUND OF OBLIGATION

III. NON-MORAL THEORIES OF CONDUCT

1. It has been held that moral judgements either (*a*) assert nothing or (*b*) assert somebody's like or dislike for certain acts and characters.

2. There is no contradiction between 'This act was wrong' and 'This act was popular' or 'I am proud of this act', so (*b*) must be false. Either therefore (*a*) is true or 'This act was wrong' asserts what it is generally meant and understood to assert.

3. The motive for suggesting that it asserts nothing is the doubt whether there really are obligations or can be known to be, since they are not verifiable in sense-experience or introspection.

4. Nor are many self-evident truths, which yet differ from unquestioned assumptions in being indubitable.

5. That there are obligations and that some things are good are truths of this kind.

6. Most who have denied the reality of obligations have been *Psychological Hedonists*, though some of these have thought obligations real.

7. The desire for my happiness upon the whole presupposes other desires which may conflict with and overcome it.

8. The doctrine gains nothing by substituting 'My own good' for 'my happiness'.

9. 'Good' preceded by a possessive or followed by a dative means advantageous; good absolutely means something different; but the two meanings are confused.

IV. CRUDE MORAL THEORIES

A. EGOISTIC HEDONISM

1. The crudest theory which allows of conflict and choice between desire and duty is *egoistic hedonism.*

2. If a man believed he had no other duty than to make himself happy, then not to torture others when he thought it would do so would cause him remorse.

3. The formula of *self-realization* only differs from this in vagueness.

4. Some have confined themselves to maintaining that 'duty and interest *coincide*'. But (*a*) if the alleged maximum happiness

4. The painfulness of a conscientious action seems to make it better but less desirable; it also lessens the goodness which consists in the proportionment of happiness to desert.

(ii) CONTEMPLATION OF GOODS

5. We can desire the existence of good things, but only the contemplation of that existence can satisfy us. We generally desire to contemplate the existence of anything, good or not, whose existence we desire.

   If the contemplation of things we think good were desired because of its own goodness, we should desire it as much in others as in ourselves, since it would be equally good.

(iii) POSSESSION OF GOODS

6. Or can we specially desire (because of their goodness) that good states or activities should occur in our own lives though they would be as good in another's? This seems self-contradictory if good is a non-relational quality. When good activities are also pleasant we desire to enjoy them.

7. The eminently good activity of conscientious action may be painful. So far, it could only be desired to exist, if at all, in all men equally.

8. If it were specially desired for oneself that must be because of some indirect pleasure in it, such as pride.

9. We have some desire that conscientious actions should occur, because good; and we can only bring them about in ourselves. We often desire something incompatible more.

10. If I think I have a duty I may go on to think that to do it for that reason would be good, and desire that this good should occur. But if I were to do it simply from this desire I should not be doing it solely because I thought it my duty and it would not have *that* goodness. The purely conscientious act would only be done either without reflection on its goodness, or when the desire aroused *by* such reflection were not so strong as one incompatible.

11. This difficulty has led to the view that because we think it optimizing we always think it our duty to do the optimizing act. If we do not think it optimific we should not think it optimizing unless we already thought of it as done because we already thought it a duty.

   An act optimizing because it is a moral act need not be for my good though done by me.

PART II

POLITICAL THINKING

XIV. MORALS AND POLITICS

(i) THE GROUND OF ALLEGIANCE

1. Political theory is a branch or application of moral theory. The rulers and those who appoint or influence them have obligations.

2. Whether we ought to obey the laws and what laws we ought to make depend on our obligations to our fellow men, those of justice, beneficence, and improvement.

3. Political obligation has sometimes been otherwise grounded: (*a*) on the General Will, an entity distinct from any number of private wills, which makes for what is good;

4. (*b*) by utilitarians, on beneficence alone;

5. (*c*) by others, solely on the justice of contract-keeping. This might conceivably cover the duties of obedience, but not those of legislation. The contract theory is unhistorical.

6. Its upholders have to resort to a tacit contract, entered into by residence or, in democracies, by voting. But citizenship is not voluntary.

7. Obligations both of obedience and of good government look mainly to the future. It is to the future that rulers and candidates appeal.

8. Individual bad laws should often be obeyed if they are part of a good system, or of any system better than anarchy.

9. The political benefits we have received were mostly from our predecessors; those we can confer are mainly to posterity.

(ii) THE IDEAL STATE

10. The best state pursues justice, beneficence, and improvement most effectively. Is there ground for thinking democracy most likely to do this? Democracy means majority rule, which may be disinterested or selfish like any other.

11. Government should be by the best and wisest. But there is no way of discovering them or of keeping them wise and good when in absolute power.

12. Election of representatives is the least improbable device for discovering an aristocracy by trial and error and for keeping it sound by criticism. A majority may contain all or most of the wise.

13. Democracy (*a*) is suited to large communities, (*b*) tends to replace violence by persuasion, and (*c*) encourages self-criticism and tolerance.

14. Democracy is a good device for preventing oppression; but it depends on freedom of speech and intelligence.

15. Apart from the probable effects, has every man a claim to share in government?

XV. THE RIGHTS OF MAN

(i) EQUALITY

1. Democracy is likely to be beneficent and still more likely to be just, i.e. to secure to the governed individuals (i.e. to the minority) their rights.

2. Every man has an equal right to have his claim to liberty, possessions, improvement, and the means of happiness considered. Perhaps he always has a right to free speech.

3. Equality is a right, to be defined by the situation, i.e. by need, desert, and use.

4. All rational beings are equally capable of morality, and to a less degree, of other goods.

5. Equality is utilitarian also.

(ii) LIBERTY

6. Men only have a right to *equal* liberty, liberty being the power to do, and so far as possible to get, what they would choose.

7. Liberty, when the word is not qualified, means *the power of doing what one would choose, unaffected by the coercion or intimidation of other persons.* It has nothing to do with moral freedom of choice. It is not legal freedom, i.e. the power of doing what the law allows.

8. Nor is it merely freedom from legal restraint, but freedom from *all* restraint by other persons.

9. Nor is it merely the power of doing what we ought. All laws restrict liberty, very often rightly.

PART I

ETHICAL THINKING

I

AIMS AND METHODS OF MORAL PHILOSOPHY

§ 1. WHY do men study moral philosophy? What do they expect from it? Do they get what they expected? Do they get anything worth getting?

Some sciences fail to achieve what those who began them hoped for, but are still pursued because they are found worth while in some unexpected way. Others are pursued for a like reason after the original aim has been attained. Astronomy may have begun in the hope that it would assist navigation and prophecy; the one objective has been taken by astronomers and the other left, and astronomy is now mostly pursued out of curiosity. Mathematics may have been first thought of as having a commercial value; later it was developed for its own sake, without suspicion of the services it was to afford both to useful and to theoretical sciences.

§ 2. Philosophy has been impressively said to have begun in wonder, a politer name for curiosity, and has been cynically said to end there. But I think moral philosophy may have begun for the race, as it often still begins for the individual, with a practical aim. Men hope both to save themselves the worry of deciding on their duties if they can discover some foolproof earmark of right and wrong, of good and evil, and they hope also to refute professed sceptics by demonstrating that obligations and goodness are realities, not merely personal tastes or superstitions. I think these hopes are generally disappointed, but yet I doubt if there are many subjects better worth studying than moral philosophy. Take first the hope of saving ourselves worry, and consider the possible meanings of asking what, in a given situation, is my duty. I might mean something so simple as 'What treatment ought I to give this invalid?' or 'Which fiscal policy ought I to vote for?' But if these questions are to be answered, it will be by medicine or economics and not by philosophy. Those sciences will tell me how I am most likely to effect a cure or to bring about prosperity and justice in my country. And if it be then asked why I should try to keep my promises or to diminish pain rather than the contrary, philosophy refuses to answer or can only reply that any answer would be as absurd as would any answer to the question why it follows that if A is larger than B and B than C, A must be larger than C. The taking of medicine is a means to health, so there is a sensible answer to the question why I should give this medicine; but the relief of a sick man need not be a means to anything, so there is no sensible answer to the question why, or for what purpose, I ought to relieve him. If it be replied that a very sensible answer would be that I should get a big fee, it must be pointed out that this does not answer the question why I *ought*, since it may be my duty to relieve the destitute and I ought not to do some things which would be well paid. It would only be an answer to some such question as what 'good' or advantage it would do me, and if it pretends to answer the question why I ought it has simply assumed that there is no such fact as duty and that men can aim at nothing but the satisfaction of their desires.

§ 3. This leads us back to the second hope which often attracts students to moral philosophy, the hope that it will demonstrate against sceptics the reality of duty and goodness: that there really are some things we ought or ought not to do, and that some characters and actions are better than others. But such demonstration must consist in deducing obligations from something more certain, and what can be more certain than that a man whom I have promised to pay for an un-

pleasant bit of work, and who has done it, has a claim to the
payment promised? This is as self-evident as the axioms
of mathematics, the law of universal causation, or the principles of logic, none of which can be proved from anything
more certain, though they are the bases of all other science.
I cannot indeed prove that other persons exist, though I
sufficiently know it, and I suggest that the fact of obligations
to them is equally sure. We can refute certain plausible
arguments in favour of moral scepticism;[1] but this does not
prove the reality of obligations, it only removes something
that seemed inconsistent with it.

§ 4. Every man who makes a promise at least professes to
believe that he thereby incurs some degree of obligation to
keep it, and the other party to the bargain only closes with
it on the like understanding; to deny this while promising
would be self-contradictory. Such obligation may indeed
conflict with some other, and we shall then have to judge
which is the stronger; for it is only the strongest present
obligation which constitutes a duty and to which a right of
the other party, as distinct from a claim, corresponds.[2]
Without the belief in this obligation the phrase 'I promise'
would be fatuous; yet we daily use it and often loyally keep
our word.

We are at least equally certain that there is really an
obligation to spare giving what I may call wanton pain, and
also one correlative to try to relieve undeserved pain. This

[1] See Ch. III.
[2] I must ask readers to note that this is the language I intend to use.
What I call 'obligations' were inaccurately called by Kant 'grounds of
duty'. They have been called by Sir David Ross 'prima facie duties'; the
objection to this is that any common prejudice or superstition or taboo
about conduct, with no foundation in moral facts, might be so called.
Professor Prichard calls them 'claims', but this word is required for the
credit rather than the debit side of the relation. I have myself in the past
called them 'responsibilities'. I now prefer the term 'obligations' and say
that when I have an obligation to a man he has a correlative claim. My
distinction is not the legal one.

obligation again may conflict with others: for instance, one to keep a promise, or to prevent crime, or to benefit the pained person or other people; and we should then have to decide which is the stronger obligation that will constitute our duty in the situation. But the things we weigh against one another in coming to such a decision are clearly not nothing. Once more, if it be asked why we ought to diminish pain rather than pleasure, however little it affects ourselves, I can only reply that I do not need any proof and that I cannot conceive of anything more certain from which it could be deduced.

§ 5. If someone who has been told that he is obliged to pay a man certain money or to give him certain drugs asks why, his question may in different contexts have different meanings and require different answers:

(1) In one context the answer would be: 'Because you promised it' or 'Because they will cure him' (assuming that you have the capacity).

(2) But if the question means 'Why ought I to keep my promise or relieve pain?' the only answer is that it is the nature of a promise to oblige us to fulfilment and of undeserved pain to oblige us to relief.

(3) If the question means 'How do I know that I am obliged?' the answer is that our reason immediately apprehends that what is assumed to be the situation[1] gives rise to obligation. Suggestions that some other faculty than reason is concerned must be considered later.[2]

Somewhat similarly, if a man asked why he should believe that A is equal to C, an answer might be that each is equal to B. But if he wanted to know why he should believe that things equal to the same thing are equal to one another, he must be content to hear that such is the nature of things, and that all this our reason immediately apprehends. If he doubts whether A or C really is equal to B, we must ulti-

[1] See Ch. II.   [2] Ch. XVII.

mately refer him to perception and admit that certainty is impossible, just as it is impossible to be certain what drug will cure or whether a man is ill.

§ 6. If, then, moral philosophy cannot prove either that we have duties or what in detail they are, it may well be asked why we study it. I think we all in some degree want, and also believe we have some obligation, to make ourselves and others capable of thinking and speaking clearly, especially about important matters such as conduct. All who have listened to discussions about morals in chance company, unused and untrained to such arguments, will know the profound dissatisfaction in which they conclude. Everybody contradicts everybody, including himself; nobody could conceal his obvious fallacies except by red herrings; misunderstandings are universal; the disputant who comes off best is the one who talks most and loudest because least aware of his own ignorance and of the intricacies in the subject. A discussion between trained thinkers will be as different from all this as a first-class match from one where the players know neither the rules nor the ropes. There will still be plenty of disagreement, but the disputants will know what they disagree about; they will understand each other's language and even the reasons for conclusions from which they differ; all parties will generally feel enlightened by the argument, and see that they have much in common. In such talks it is far more usual to hear 'I believe after all you are right', or at least 'There is something in what you say'.

§ 7. The cause of this improvement is that in moral philosophy we learn to use language with much greater care and discrimination. In ordinary talk, where no great consistency or accuracy is expected, we use terms like 'right', 'moral', 'virtuous', 'good', 'meritorious', 'obligatory', as if they all meant much the same; but when we have to speak accurately we find that actions and characters can be ethically commended on different grounds, and that we must either invent new words to indicate these differences or select which among the names we have hitherto used loosely is most appropriate to each. Even popular language begins to recognize this when it is said that an opponent is acting wrongly though honestly; that 'an honest man is the noblest work of God' though honesty is merely the best policy. Moral philosophy distinguishes the ethical from the non-ethical meaning of terms and also one ethical meaning from another.

§ 8. Is the benefit of moral philosophy, then, purely intellectual and in no degree practical? I think that it does not and should not affect our conduct directly, for like other sciences it has no other basis than our apprehension of the facts and we must not juggle with facts to support our theory. If a moral philosopher's arguments led to practical precepts directly contradictory to men's reflective conclusions on simple moral questions, we should have the best possible reason for thinking that he was in error, that he had either argued fallaciously or assumed false premisses. In our most ordinary casuistry we have already embarked for an ethics; our more considered judgements are the philosopher's only data; and if he pretends to contradict them except by still more careful analysis of their meaning, he is like an astronomer who should declare a crescent moon gibbous because it must be so by his cosmology.

§ 9. Philosophy, then, can only clarify our ethical thinking and help us to avoid taking for granted that uncriticized taboos or prejudices or fashions are moral judgements. The case is similar with logic, which can neither contradict nor confirm our immediate certainty that if all A is B and all B is C, all A is C, but may remind us of our uncertainty about the premisses, and by analysing more complicated arguments help us to see that they are only specious fallacies, though in the end we must see it for ourselves.

So there comes about an indirect influence of moral

philosophy upon conduct. Every sane person has done some
moral philosophizing, but since most of us are intellectually
lazy, if he has not been specially stimulated, this probably
consisted in accepting high-sounding generalities of other
people, who may either have been as superficial as himself
or had some axe to grind. And for bad philosophy the only
cure is better.

§ 10. To take a crude instance; the theory has found
favour that a man's only duty is to make himself as happy as
possible, but I do not think its disciples have often been
pedantic enough to act on it or to distort their particular
judgements accordingly. Like other men they either followed
their uncontaminated moral reason or consciously disobeyed
while believing it. But in some sharp conflict between desire
and conscience, the recollection of the academic dogma may
have reinforced their selfish prudence and encouraged them
in bad behaviour.[1]

§ 11. Or again it has been held that the sole duty is to
increase the general amount of happiness, and a man who
accepted this plausible doctrine may sometimes have used it
to stifle his conviction that he owed money to a creditor who
seemed to need it less than himself.

§ 12. As a last and more subtle instance: it is often said that
men have no freedom of choice but inevitably 'make the
choice' which is determined by their inborn nature, history,
and environment. As a rule, I think, the holders of this
doctrine make efforts to choose rightly, and also feel remorse
when they have chosen wrongly, exactly like other men;
which at least suggests some scepticism of the doctrine. But
sometimes in a moral crisis a man may have said to himself:
'Well, since I have to make just the effort and just the
decision I do make, and which anybody who really knew me
would know I must make, why worry about either the past
or future? Or rather I suppose I must worry as much as I

---

[1] Cf. F. H. Bradley, *Mr. Sidgwick's Hedonism*, p. 50.

must and cannot worry more.' And this may have led him to try less than he otherwise would.

§ 13. In all these cases conduct may have been influenced by crude theories which have been absorbed from popular books or sermons—perhaps unconsciously—by people who hardly suspected they were 'philosophizing'. And if this has happened there is only one cure; the antidote to loose thinking is nothing but closer thinking:

> A little learning is a dangerous thing;
> Drink deep, or taste not the Pierian spring.

I am far from suggesting that there was ever a golden age of pure moral judgement later contaminated by the perversity of sophists. As soon as a child's mind is sufficiently developed to understand the word 'ought', it is already subject to nursery propaganda. As the human mind developed from animal instinct it had to struggle against old habits and patterns of behaviour. All I would maintain is that at any stage of mental development a man will be at least as likely to make true moral judgements[1] if he candidly applies his mind to the situation as if he starts with some general rule or theory; but since in fact he always does so start, though he usually twists it to fit either his desires or his conscience, he may indirectly improve his conduct by improving his theory, by reaching one which is a truer generalization of the verdicts of reflective conscience upon particular situations. Good philosophy is a prophylactic against bad philosophy, a poison which is always in our systems.

§ 14. The main purpose of moral philosophy, however, is to analyse and clarify our moral thinking; and consequently we must distinguish this moral thinking, which is its subject-matter, from other subjects. Moral thinking is obviously thinking about the meaning of such words as

---

[1] i.e. to judge correctly what action is morally demanded by the situation. See next Chapter.

'right', 'obligation', 'good', 'merit', and their opposites; but we have to recognize that it is not concerned with all the meanings of all these words, since some of them are used in non-ethical as well as ethical meaning: 'The *right* way to get rich quickly is to do some actions which are not *right*'; 'You *ought* not to be so scrupulous if you want to succeed'; 'A *good* man does not always have a *good* time; he thinks about other things than his own *good*.' So not only have various ethical meanings of such words to be distinguished from one another but also their ethical from their non-ethical meanings.

There are, of course, many other words besides the ethical which are used ambiguously, metaphorically, or analogously, but most of them are less likely to be misunderstood. Nobody thinks that a high note or number or ideal is a long way above the ground, but people do sometimes suppose that 'a right act' must mean the right way to achieve some advantage, such as happiness or honour, which does not always seem true; as they also suppose that what is good must be for the 'good' or advantage of the person who calls it so, or at least for that of the majority, which is very questionable. A right act is merely the right way to do right, that is, our duty, and a good act is equally good whoever does it and whomever it may benefit. If we may infer that when Christ prayed the cross might be spared him he believed that he was forsaken of God and betrayed by his friends, and that the cause for which he had sacrificed himself and his followers was ruined and mistaken, we must conclude that he was eminently good but thought he had not attained his own good or that of anybody else.

I have tried to say shortly, and in a general way, what I take to be the chief aim and subject of moral philosophy; and in doing so I have naturally given some indication of what I take to be its usual method. This is to define or discriminate the meanings of various terms and phrases commonly used in the commendation or censure of characters and actions, and to check these distinctions by instances. But this raises a troublesome logical difficulty about definition.

§ 15. If somebody defines the usual meaning of the word 'justice' as obedience to the laws of your country, I might contest his definition[1] by asserting some laws to be so bad that it is unjust to obey them, and to this he might reply that here was precisely where we differed and that I was simply begging the question. All I could do would be to ask him to ponder candidly whether he thinks it just to beat all Jews or all fair-haired men in one country and unjust in another, whether the laws of both countries are equally just, and whether there is no justice in matters not statutable. Somewhat similarly, if he said that 'high notes' meant those made by wind instruments, I should simply ask if he could not recognize a quality common to certain given notes whether of wind or strings, and should explain that this is what in the context is generally meant by 'high'. If he could not recognize this common quality, I should think his ear defective, and, since justice is not observed by eye or ear, if he failed to recognize the distinction between just and unjust laws it would be his reason that I should think deficient. I might try to convince him that there really is a difference between high and low notes other than that of timbre, by referring to differences of vibration; and similarly that there really is a difference between 'justice' and 'injustice' other than legality by trying to indicate some other quality or relation common and peculiar to all just acts and laws which is the ground of their being just.

[1] 'We should not be searching for the definition if we already knew precisely the meaning of the term; but the fact that we accept a certain definition as correct shows that we think the definition expresses more clearly the very thing we had in mind when we used the term without knowing its definition. The correctness of a definition is tested by two methods: by asking (i) whether the denotation of the term and that of the proposed definition are the same; (ii) does the definition express explicitly what we had implicitly in mind when we used the term?' (Ross, *Foundations of Ethics*.)

§ 16. This, in fact, has been one of the chief objects of moral philosophers: to discover some other character or relation common to all the acts we ought to do which is the reason why we ought to do them. It is conceivable there might be some such common ground, but we cannot assume that there must be, any more than we can assume that there is one common ground from which we could deduce the truth of all statements, say, of '2 × 2 = 4' and 'I am now writing'. To suggest that both are in accordance with facts is not to name any common character other than their truth: it is simply what we mean by truth, as to say that justice is giving every man his due is merely to repeat the term 'justice' in a paraphrase. It has indeed been held that, as it is impossible to define such simple things as colour or feeling, so it is impossible to define duty or goodness without using moral terms which imply them, since they too are simple and ultimate.[1]

As I have hinted, a chief reason for the obstinate effort to find a common non-ethical character in all obligations or in all good things is the desire to escape the trouble of using our moral judgement. If it could be clearly shown that obligatory acts have some peculiar character, either immediately perceived such as being the most attractive to the agent, or probably inferred such as conducing to his ultimate satisfaction or to the survival of his species, then it would be possible for a man utterly lacking conscience to know how ordinary people would apply the words 'good' and 'ought'. So, too, a man born stone-deaf who could observe vibrations might know which notes would be called high, but he could never know what this meant.

§ 17. In the same spirit writers on aesthetic, both ancient and modern, have asked what other quality common and peculiar to all the things we call beautiful is the ground of their beauty. Some have answered, 'Size and Pattern',[2]

---

[1] Moore, *Principia Ethica*, § 10. [2] Aristotle, *Poetics*, vii.

others, 'Unity in Variety',[1] others, 'Union of Form and Matter'.[2] But since every perceptible complex whole, however ugly, must have size and some arrangement of its parts, though not necessarily repetitive, some unity in variety, and some union of form and matter, none of these can be the ground of beauty, and we are entitled to ask what size or patterns, what forms or materials, what unities or varieties are beautiful. And the usual answers, such as 'The Symmetrical' or 'The Harmonious', only repeat 'Beauty' in less colloquial words.

Others tried to give a more precise criterion: 'The most beautiful line is serpentine';[3] 'The most beautiful shape is a rectangle two of whose sides are in proportion 21 : 34 to the other two';[4] 'A good play keeps the unities of time and place';[5] 'A good novel is one which makes its readers better'.[6] All these criteria could be measured or in some way verified by an observer with absolutely no artistic appreciation; yet it is paradoxical to suggest that he could really know what would be the experience of beauty for those better endowed. And even if these qualities were precisely the ones that caused that experience, they could not be what we mean by beauty or even by a species of it, since it is significant to ask: 'Is an improving novel always beautiful literature?' So, too, it is significant to ask whether beneficent acts, or those with survival value, are alone or even always right.

§ 18. Just as we can often tell of any actual picture what element, say, its colour or its line, makes us admire it, so we can distinguish in a situation what element is the ground of some particular goodness or obligation, but it seems impossible to find one common ground for all instances or to elucidate the meaning of either word, and any attempt to do

[1] Coleridge, *On the Principles of Sound Criticism.*
[2] Plotinus, *Enneads,* x.   [3] Hogarth, *Analysis of Beauty.*
[4] Fechner, *Vorschule der Aesthetik.*
[5] Corneille, *Des Trois Unités.*
[6] Tolstoy, *What is Art?* These last four citations are all summaries.

so without using ethical terms has been called the 'natural-istic' fallacy[1] though perhaps 'heterogeneous' would be a better adjective. If we defined obligation as the keeping of promises, the definition would be not only too narrow but circular, since promise is an ethical term which can only be explained as bringing oneself under an obligation of a particular sort.

In this attempt to sketch the purpose, subject, and method of moral philosophy I have had to touch upon many of the controversies whose more careful consideration will occupy most of the following chapters.

[1] Moore, *Principia Ethica*, § 10, &c.

II

THE GROUND OF OBLIGATION

§ 1. BEFORE trying to classify our obligations by asking whether they are all founded on one ground or on two or more, it is necessary to consider the general nature of a ground of obligation. Unfortunately this is a puzzling and not very interesting question, but the looseness of our ordinary language on the subject has caused much philosophical confusion which has been seldom noticed. The general question is whether our obligations, and consequently our duties, depend upon our actual situation, including our capacities for affecting it and the consequences of what we may immediately bring about, or upon our beliefs about that situation, or upon our moral estimate of what the supposed situation demands. The first view, that obligations depend on the real situation, has been called the objective view; the second, that they depend on our beliefs about it, the subjective; and the third, that they depend upon our estimate of what is morally demanded by the supposed situation, I venture to call the putative view.[1]

In our everyday language we unconsciously imply all these views. We say: 'You really ought to give him quinine

[1] For the whole question see Prichard, *Duty and Ignorance of Fact*, and Ross, *The Right and the Good*, pp. 41–7, and *The Foundations of Ethics*, vii. Professor Broad (in *Philosophy*, July 1946) calls my putative obligation 'subjective', and my objective and subjective severally 'material' and 'formal' on the analogy of materially true conclusions and those formally correct, i.e. correctly drawn from false premisses. I am much indebted to discussions with Professor Prichard for clearing up my confusion. Unfortunately we could not agree. Richard Price perhaps first noticed the question in his *Review of the Principal Questions in Morals*. He calls the objective view 'abstract' and the subjective and putative, without clear distinction, 'practical', practical duties being what a man ought to do 'upon supposition of his having such and such sentiments of things', these being 'produced by the different application of the same principles'.

because he really has malaria' or 'You really ought to repay him because you borrowed'; and this implies the objective view. We also say: 'A doctor ought to give whatever drug he thinks most likely to cure what he thinks is the patient's illness', or 'In such a case he ought not to have risked an operation, though it succeeded', which implies the subjective view. And we also say: 'A man ought to pay what he thinks fair', 'A man ought always to obey his conscience'; and this implies the putative view.

§ 2. But if the words 'ought', 'obligation', 'duty' are used with strictly the same sense in these three ways, only one of the views can be true. It cannot be true that at the same moment a man ought, in the same sense, to give his last crust to A and also to B, yet either act might be any of these three so-called duties. Obligations can, of course, conflict, but not duties;[1] and when obligations conflict they can be compared, but an objective obligation could not be compared with a putative, for, if I knew both, they would coincide, being only differentiated by ignorance or error.

Are the words then used in different senses in the three different contexts? When we do use the word 'ought' in a sense clearly different from 'strongest immediate obligation' it is possible to distinguish this sense by a paraphrase without using the word or any synonym: in the sentence 'You ought not to have trumped that card'[2] (as distinct from 'You ought not to be playing cards'), the former can be translated: 'Your assumed desire of winning would have been satisfied by trumping', or 'Trumping caused your disappointment'. Similarly, 'We ought soon (or now) to be in sight of land' means 'If our calculations, or the time-table, are correct, we shall soon see land' (or 'Since we cannot see land there was an error'). But if while holding any one of

---

[1] If two incompatible and indivisible obligations were precisely equal, a man's duty would be to do either (whichever he please).

[2] Kant's 'hypothetical imperative' or 'imperative of technique'.

these three theories we say that, in phrases implying either of the other two, 'ought', 'obligation', 'duty' are used in a different sense, we find it hard to paraphrase them without using the same word or a synonym. Thus a supporter of the objective view will say that 'subjective duty' means 'what a man *ought* to do if the situation were what he supposes', and that 'putative duty' means 'what a man thinks he *ought* to do'. A supporter of the subjective view will say that 'objective duty' means 'what a man *ought* to do if he had knowledge of the situation', and so on.

§ 3. Yet it is hard to say that any of these applications is incorrect, for the proper 'use' of a word is the 'usual' one in which it is usually understood, and these three uses seem about equally common. Granting, however, that we do, when not reflecting, apply the words inconsistently, it may be asked in which way we should apply them after criticism and reflection. To answer this question we must summarize the arguments used on each side.

(1) In favour of the putative view it is urged that only on this view could a man certainly know what is his duty or whether he has done it. Not being historically omniscient, he cannot know all the past relations of the parties concerned; not being scientifically omniscient, he can never know all the consequences of what he can immediately bring about;[1] not being psychologically omniscient, he cannot know the capacities of himself or others to affect the situation. Yet all these things of which he is ignorant are relevant elements in the situation he has to deal with. He can, on the objective view, only do his duty by luck, and this we are at first very unwilling to admit. So far the argument has only aimed at precluding the objective view. But further, a man, not being morally infallible, cannot certainly know whether some

[1] If we accept freedom of choice (see Ch. XII), presumably omniscience itself could not tell what use would be made by moral beings of the situations or subjective situations in which it placed them.

factor in the situation as he believes it to be may not involve an obligation which he has overlooked or which is really stronger than one he has over-estimated. So the argument is equally valid against the subjective view. It is only his putative duty that a man can certainly know. It is only for doing or neglecting this that he could be held morally responsible.

(2) The holders of the subjective view press this same argument strongly against the objective view, but do not seem to admit that it is equally damaging to their own. Against the putative view they urge the absurdity of maintaining that whatever a man thinks to be his duty is his duty.[1] What could be the meaning of 'thinking something *to be* my duty' if whatever I thought so was so? The view would amount to a denial of all obligation.

(3) Those who favour the objective view rely mainly on two arguments:

(*a*) They point out that only on this view can it be true, as we commonly suppose, that in actions affecting others a duty of the agent always corresponds to a right of the patient, and an obligation to a claim, being the other end of the same stick.[2] Whereas if my duty to pay you depended on my fallible memory, and your right on yours, the two need by no means correspond. The creditor who said: 'You *really* ought to pay me because, though you do not think so, you borrowed'

[1] See the last paragraph of this section.

[2] The most obvious exceptions suggested are the alleged disobligations to cannibalism (by starving persons, like Conrad's *Secret Sharer*, of those accidentally dead), to homosexuality, and to incest. The 'natural horror' which causes them to be called 'sins against nature' makes it hard to judge if they are morally wrong because in the long run detrimental, or merely disgusting either to a certain civilization, as are polygamy and mixed marriages, or to our inexperience, as is the first sight of operations and dissections. The cases of obligations to ourselves will be considered in Ch. X. I have a natural horror of cruelty, but here there *is* a correlative claim. The difficulty of finding rights correlative to the alleged duties of punishment and of prudence will be discussed in Chs. V and X. I see no difficulty in attributing rights to animals.

would be saying what was not true.[1] And since it takes two to make a promise, the same *mutatis mutandis* is true of the other party's acceptance. A man who said 'You really do not owe it me, because, though you do not think so, I refused the bargain' would be saying what was not true. On this view I could always give a man a duty or deprive him of a right by a lie if he believed me.

(*b*) If a man's real duty depended upon his beliefs about the situation, it is hard to see why we all think that we ought[2] to consider the circumstances and its moral implications as fully as possible. The result of doing so would only be to substitute one duty for another, and the new duty would be no more a duty than the old.[3]

Perhaps the strongest argument against the objective view is that, on it, it is hard to say why we do not think infants or animals or, for that matter, sticks and stones have obligations.[4]

---

[1] Ross, who in his *Foundations of Ethics* rejects the objective view, seems to forget this on p. 19, where he says that our common differences about duties throw doubt 'not on the *fundamental* [my italics] moral judgment . . . but on the opinions about ordinary fact'. And again on p. 139 he paraphrases with approval Aristotle, *Eth. Nic.* 1105^b 8, as follows: 'The whole content of . . . that which it is incumbent on us to do . . . is described . . . as arising from the nature of the situation . . . i.e. from the rights of the various persons affected.' And again on p. 289 he assumes that A's duty to B and B's right from A are identical. However much inclined we may sometimes be to pitch the objective view overboard, yet it always creeps back.

[2] For this use of 'ought' see § 5 below.

[3] Prichard's answer to this (*Duty and Ignorance of Fact*, p. 15), if I understand it, really undermines his own argument for the subjective view. It concludes by admitting that our 'duty is one of the full nature of which we are at the time inevitably ignorant owing to our ignorance of the facts'. But since we shall always be ignorant of some relevant facts we can never know our duty.

[4] But see Ch. XIII, § 2. I can only suggest here that infants and animals, unlike savages, have not the thought of obligation; and are therefore incapable of free choice or, in the strict sense, of action. But obligation is to an act of choice. The savage, in divination and consultation of oracles, sometimes recognizes an obligation to seek for other obligations.

Some of these difficulties are evaded by substituting for the absolute words 'ought', 'obligation', 'duty' relative words like 'suitable' or 'fitting'. One act I might do would be fitting (by luck) to the actual situation, another (if I had moral acumen and were conscientious) to my belief about the situation, and a third (if I were conscientious though morally insensitive) to my estimate of what was fitting to the situation as I believed it to be.[1] But is this more than evasion? The question still remains: Which of the three imagined acts, suitable severally to X, Y, Z, is the man's duty?

§ 4. I will try to give an account of the matter so far as it is possible to give one which I hope would be accepted by all parties to the dispute. In our unreflective moments we all commonly take it for granted or assume without question that we are in a certain situation (or relation to other persons) and that we have the capacity to alter (or perhaps to maintain) this situation. And we often go on to assume that it is our duty to exercise this capacity. A sentry might unquestioningly assume that he saw a wounded comrade whom he could rescue, and might assume, also without question, that he ought to do so. But experience teaches that such assumptions are very precarious, and on second thoughts he may believe that his first duty, though a derivative one, is to consider as carefully as time permits the chances that the man may be an enemy shamming, or that any attempt to rescue must fail, or even the possibility that he is himself utterly benumbed by cold. And reflection further assures him that not only was his original assumption precarious, but that the

---

[1] Ross, *Foundations of Ethics*, viii. This avoids the absurdity of saying that whatever a man thinks his duty is his duty, and only asserts that a certain possible act would be 'morally suitable to the agent's opinion on the moral question' (p. 162), i.e. is the act he thinks he ought to do. The terms 'correct act', 'appropriate act', and 'becoming' or 'behoving act' have also been suggested. In some languages there seems a wider choice if no more discrimination: *il faut, il me faut, je dois*; *Verbindung, Pflicht, Sollen*; gerundive, *oportet, decet*; δεῖ, χρῆ, προσήκει: but I would not venture beyond my native tongue.

conclusion drawn from it about his duty was fallible; even if the man were a wounded comrade whom he could rescue, it may really have been his duty to remain at his post, and this reflection may lead him to think that it is his first duty to consider whether the obligation to rescue a comrade or to retain his post is the stronger. It is only for acting in accordance with his moral judgement upon what the situation, as he believes it to be, demands, whether his judgement and belief depend upon naïve assumption or upon consideration and reflection, that he can be praised or blamed. Nobody can ever certainly know all the relevant facts of the real situation, including his own capacity for affecting it and the results of so doing. And on many, if not all, occasions, it is impossible to know one's duty even in an assumed or believed situation. Some adults are commonly aware of their fallibility in all these respects, and can therefore be blamed for not fulfilling their putative duty to give them the fullest further consideration which the case allows.

§ 5. So much I take to be common ground; but differences immediately begin. I am inclined, though with some misgivings, to say that a man's real duty depends on the real situation, and that only so long as he was assuming a knowledge of the situation and moral infallibility would he claim to know that he had done his duty, but on reflection would substitute some such phrase as 'I tried to do it' or 'I think I did it'. If he still persisted in claiming knowledge I should think he must be talking of duty on the putative view. What he may claim to know is that *if* a situation is of a certain kind it must give rise to certain *obligations*, and occasionally he may know that it is of a certain kind, or at least contains a certain element, which gives rise to an obligation. Thus he may know that he is feeling spiteful and that he has some obligation to exert himself to cure this. But there may be other and unknown elements in the real situation giving rise to an incompatible and stronger obligation, and there may be elements, even in the situation as he believes it to be, giving rise to such an obligation though he is blind to it; so for both reasons he may always be mistaken about his duty on any except the putative theory.

Further I am inclined to suggest that when we say a man ought carefully to consider the situation and its moral implications we *are* using the word 'ought' in a different sense from that in which we say he ought to do what the real situation really demands; we are using it in a sense somewhat analogous to that in which we say that a man who is trying to win ought to trump a particular card. The important difference is that what he is now trying to do is his real duty, or at least to approximate to that, so that the most likely means to succeed in his attempt carries a kind of derivative obligation. Thus, too, we say: 'Since (or assuming that) I ought to visit this sick man as soon as possible, I *think* I ought to spend a few minutes consulting time-tables'; for though this might lose me the first train, it is the most probable method of arriving quickly. I agree that a man cannot have a duty to do what is impossible, but I have only allowed that he has duties of which he must be ignorant, so that he *can* do them 'by accident' or, if he is trying to do them (and in the first place to discover them), 'by luck'. It is for trying that he is responsible.[1]

I do not think it of vital importance in which of the three customary ways we apply the words 'duty', 'ought',

[1] I believe I am here in substantial agreement with Sir David Ross (*Foundations of Ethics*, p. 207), who says: 'What (the good man) desires primarily to do is his objective duty. But, knowing the difficulty of knowing what act will be the doing of his objective duty, i.e. will produce the effect (of relieving a sick man) he also has a secondary desire, the desire to do his subjective duty, i.e. the act which he thinks to be his objective duty. . . . This conscientious action is adopting means to an end.' For reasons given in Ch. XII I should not use the word 'desire' here. What is called subjective duty and identified with conscientious action I should call putative duty. Instead of 'thinks to be his objective duty' I should say 'thinks to approximate to' it.

obligation'; I cannot think of any results in our subsequent discussions which would be affected. What is vitally important is not to confuse the three applications as is commonly done.

I shall therefore continue for brevity to use the phrases 'objective duty', by which I mean a man's real duty (though those who differ from me must translate it 'what would be a man's duty if he were infallible'); 'subjective duty', by which I mean 'what would be a man's duty if the situation were what he supposes' (though they must translate it 'his real duty'); and 'putative duty', by which I mean 'what a man thinks his duty'. And I repeat that the last alone is what a man can know and for doing or neglecting which he can be praised or blamed.

§ 6. I said we can never know our subjective duty but only a subjective obligation. We may know that, *if* the situation is as we believe, we have an obligation to pay certain money; but it is always conceivable that some factor in the believed situation may really be the ground of an incompatible stronger obligation, though we fail either to recognize this obligation at all or to recognize its superior strength.

It seems that only if we sometimes know a subjective obligation can we properly be said to know that there are objective ones at all. If all we could ever say were that, supposing the situation to be as we believed, we *think* it would involve some obligation or other (i.e. we have a putative obligation),[1] it is hard to see what knowledge about the reality of obligations could be derived from this or presupposed by it. But if we may truly say that, supposing the situation to be as we believe, we know that it would oblige us to a certain action, then this implies that a situation of a certain kind always carries an obligation of some degree, and, if this is so, we know certain general principles of objective obligation whose probable application to supposed situations gives rise to subjective obligations, the estimate of whose

---

[1] But see § 5 above.

several degrees gives rise to putative duties. And only if we know there are objective obligations, though we can never be quite certain what in a given situation they are, can we ever know, as I hold we can, some of our subjective obligations.

§ 7. Our subjective duty can only be to try to effect or prevent a certain change when we think either possible, since we can never be sure of our success; even the limb we try to move may have gone to sleep or become paralysed. An objective duty would never be to try but always to effect or to prevent; an omniscient being would know whether he was able[1] or not, and it would not be his duty to try the impossible. So objective and subjective duties never strictly coincide.

In one sense we cannot try to do our objective duty since we do not know what it is. But if under the phrase 'trying to do' we include trying to get better grounded opinions of what our objective duty is so that we may be less likely to act very wrongly, then this is often a putative duty. It certainly cannot be an objective one and may not be a subjective one. It cannot be an objective duty, for that depends on an actual situation independently of my subjective beliefs or doubts about it. Nor need it be a subjective one; my opinion about the situation might give rise to two conflicting subjective obligations, one to inquire into the situation further and the other to act at once, and the stronger of these would be my subjective duty. But I might falsely think the other to be the stronger and then it would be my putative but not my subjective duty. A general's opinion about the enemy's strength might give rise to conflicting subjective obligations, one to attack at once, as more likely to secure victory, the other to reconnoitre the defences, as more likely to save his men. One is presumably his subjective duty, but he might not think so.

---

[1] Though he would know that he was only able if he 'tried' in the sense of 'setting himself to do' (cf. Prichard, *Duty and Ignorance of Fact*). If not free he might know if he was going to 'try'.

§ 8. The actual or objective situation, about which we may be very ignorant, may give rise to certain objective obligations, some of which may be incompatible so that we cannot fulfil them all; yet it seems strange to speak of an objective obligation we cannot fulfil. I think it would be improper to speak of an obligation we *could* not fulfil *if we tried*, such as to move in two directions at once or to learn Chinese in a week, but we might have an obligation (objective or subjective) which we could not try to fulfil because either (*a*) we may not think it an obligation (i.e. it is not a putative obligation) and may not desire to do the action, and we cannot choose to do what we neither desire nor think obligatory,[1] or (*b*) though we thought it an obligation, we might think we had a stronger obligation which was incompatible and which we more desired or less disliked to fulfil.

What a man can always do is to fulfil a putative duty. He can always try to bring about a result which he thinks he ought to try to bring about, for if he could think of no way of trying he could not think it his duty to try. We might make this clearer to ourselves in an illustration. I have in fact promised to pay a man some money on Tuesday. If I meet him on Tuesday evening, have the money in my pocket and am not paralysed, I have some degree of objective obligation to pay him now, for I can do so if I try. But (*a*) if I do not desire to pay him now and believe I promised to pay him next Tuesday, I cannot try to pay him now. Or (*b*) if I do not desire to pay him now and, though I believe I promised to pay him this Tuesday, also believe I have a stronger and incompatible obligation to use the money otherwise, again I cannot try to pay him now. I probably at first take for granted that my belief of having promised to pay next Tuesday is correct and that therefore if I can pay him next Tuesday it will then be my objective duty to do so. And, I suppose, if it simply does not occur to me (probably through

[1] See Ch. XI, §§ 5, 6.

having been unscrupulous about my duties in the past) that my memory is fallible and that I am apt to overlook obligations less publicly advertised than debts, I cannot be said to have the putative duty of trying to verify either my recollection of the promise or my assumption that I have no stronger incompatible obligation; so my putative duty is to try to pay next Tuesday, e.g. to make a note of it, to 'impress it on my memory' to look at my note, to keep ready money available, and so on.

§ 9. If we suppose for a moment that the law is just, it is often the duty of a judge or jury in a civil case to try to discover the objective duty of one party and the correlative objective right of the other, for, when two or more parties are concerned,[1] objective rights and duties are always correlative—the two ends of the same stick.

In a criminal case, however, or whenever penalty and not mere damage or restitution is to be assessed, the judge and jury may also have to consider what was the subjective duty of the accused, since they may have to distinguish unavoidable ignorance, negligence, intent to injure, and intent to kill.

Occasionally, as in the case of a conscientious objector, or of malicious slander, or of some political crimes, the tribunal may even be empowered to consider putative duties, that is, not only what the accused thought about the situation but what he thought that situation morally obliged him to do.

The admitted fact that both parties to a suit may be honest men shows that neither subjectively nor putatively are rights and duties correlative. If A believes B lent him money which B believes was given, it is A's subjective duty to repay it and neither has a subjective right to it. If their beliefs about the situation were interchanged, A thinking that B gave him the money and B that it was lent, both would have a subjective right to it and neither any subjective duty.

[1] Cf. Ch. X, § 2.

§ 10. My conclusion, then, is that we always know our putative duty, sometimes a subjective obligation, but our objective duties never. A being fallible about historical and scientific fact but with infallible moral insight (which I suppose to be the orthodox conception of Christ) would always know his subjective duty since it would coincide with his putative duty, but only if he became altogether omniscient would he know his objective duty, for then only would his subjective and objective duty coincide. For a being, on the other hand, with imperfect moral insight but omniscience about historical and scientific facts, there would be coincidence between subjective and objective duty, but not between subjective and putative.

It is only for doing or neglecting a putative duty, that is, something thought to be a subjective duty and merely assumed or hoped to be an objective duty, that we would praise or blame a man, for this only could he know that he was doing or neglecting. And only for failure to do such acts could he feel remorse as distinct from regret.

§ 11. But do we always praise a man for doing his putative duty? Evidently not, for we have further to consider his motive. I may believe my situation to be one which makes it my duty to pay certain money, and I may pay it not because of this belief but because I fear punishment or loss of credit, or because I desire to borrow a larger sum which I mean to keep, and then I deserve no praise; I have not acted morally, though I have done my putative and perhaps my subjective and possibly my objective duty. It seems best to keep the word 'moral' for conscientious acts done *because* they are putative duties, and these alone deserve praise, and have *moral* goodness. A man who, from whatever motive, has done what we think was his real duty may be said to have acted rightly; but only if his motive was a good one is he or his act good.[1]

---

[1] Ross, *The Right and the Good.* But see Ch. XII, § 11, below.

§ 12. But do all such acts deserve praise? This question brings us to the conception of merit,[1] and the merit of moral action seems to depend on its difficulty. A judge may decide for one litigant against another purely because he thinks the evidence before him morally requires it, but if he has no interest in either party he has no difficulty and I should not say he had any choice, since once he has made up his mind on the evidence, no other course in any way appeals to him; he ceases to merit praise. Merit is certainly in part proportionate to the strength of the temptation resisted; whether it is also affected by the strength of the putative obligation fulfilled is not so clear; some have held it is greater where the obligation is strong and some the reverse.[2] The demerit or guilt of neglecting a putative obligation is certainly greater when the obligation is stronger and also when the temptation is weaker. Unless obligations differed in strength we could not decide which constituted a duty when they conflicted; but the putatively strongest, which constitutes a putative duty, need not be very strong.

[1] See Ch. V.   [2] R. Price, *Review*.

III

NON-MORAL THEORIES OF CONDUCT[1]

§ 1. BEFORE attempting to discover any one common ground or several grounds for our various obligations which may make them such, we must discuss a little further the denial that there really is any obligation or anything good. Such a denial would persuade us to abandon some of our commonest expressions except in the sense in which we still speak of witchcraft, or the music of the spheres, or starry influence, as names for exploded delusions, or in the sense in which we say that food is nicer when you are hungry; and this might seem too fantastic for serious consideration. But we have the statement of Locke that 'Good and evil are nothing but pleasure or pain. Morally good and evil, then, is only conformity or disagreement of our voluntary actions to some law, whereby good or evil (i.e. pleasure or pain) is drawn on us from the will and power of the law-maker, which . . . is that we call reward and punishment.'[2]

Perhaps the crudest version of the doctrine is that 'whatever is the object of any man's appetite or desire, that is it which he for his part calleth good'.[3] But since we commonly speak of bad desires, both in ourselves and others, not meaning merely that they are weak or transitory, this had to be amended by the 'moral sense school', which made goodness a matter of 'taste'.[4] It will, however, be convenient to start

---

[1] The first two sections of this chapter are in great part reproduced, with the editor's permission, from my article in *Philosophy*, April 1938.

[2] *Essay concerning Human Understanding*, II. xxviii. Yet it is only thought a duty to obey God because his laws are thought the surest guide to justice and beneficence. Cf. R. Price, *Review*, and Lamont, *Principles of Moral Judgement*, ii, § 44.

[3] Hobbes, *Leviathan*, vi.

[4] I think Hume would have accepted this for his 'moral sentiment'. Hutcheson's 'moral sense' was meant to be a special faculty, but is of a suspicious kind. Cf. Ch. XVII, § 7.

with a contemporary version and, by tracing it to its genesis, show that it is a last-ditch cemetery.

Mr. Ayer[1] says: 'Sentences which simply express moral judgments do not say anything. They are pure expressions of feeling and as such do not come under the category of truth and falsehood. . . . Aesthetic terms are used in exactly the same way as ethical terms.'

This, I think, is one instance of a tendency to confuse the facts of moral and aesthetic experience which has been disastrous for both ethics and aesthetics. Its direct parentage is confessedly to be found in Hume with his famous saying that 'Morality is more properly felt than judged of', by which I suppose he means that what we call moral judgements would more properly be described as statements about or expressions of feeling. Butler, when controverting such views in the *Preface* to the Sermons, traces the confusion back to Shaftesbury in the aphorism that 'Beauty and Good (which in the context seems to mean moral goodness) are still the same'.[2] Butler says:

'The not taking into consideration the authority [i.e. obligation] which is implied in the idea of reflex approbation or disapprobation seems a material deficiency in Lord Shaftesbury's *Inquiry Concerning Virtue* (Bk. I, Pt. III, § iii; *Characteristics*, ii, p. 69). . . . Take in then that authority and obligation which is a constituent part of this reflex approbation, and it will undeniably follow, though a man should doubt of everything else, yet, that he would still remain under the nearest and most certain obligation to the practice of virtue.'

I want first to consider the view, surely a paradox in terms, that 'moral judgments or the sentences expressing them do not say anything'. For those who hold this cannot be expected to listen patiently to a discussion whether moral judgements say something (as Hume thought) about feelings

---

[1] *Language, Truth and Logic*, p. 161.
[2] *The Moralists*, Pt. III, § ii. 67.

or about some other facts, and if the latter whether they are ever true. If it can be shown that this view of Mr. Ayer is groundless and that moral judgements do assert something, it would be possible to go on to argue next that what they assert is not a state of mind of their maker or of anybody else, and lastly that they can be true. Indeed, if Mr. Ayer's view that 'moral judgments assert nothing' can be refuted, we should have already converted at least him to the view that they assert something other than the existence of feelings. For he tells us that he was at first attracted by the view that moral judgements are really statements about somebody's state of feeling, and only when he saw this view to be clearly untenable, resorted to his own paradox as the sole remaining escape from what he calls 'an absolutist view of ethics which would undermine the whole of his main argument'.[1] And if it can be shown not only that moral judgements assert something, but that what they assert is (as Mr. Ayer agrees) no state of anybody's mind, but rather a fact independent of anybody's thought or feeling about it, we might finally maintain that there is no reason to doubt that such assertions are sometimes true. Aesthetic judgements, assertions, i.e. that things are beautiful, also, I think, generally *mean* to attribute to the thing a quality independent of anybody's thoughts or feelings. But so far as they do assert this, there are reasons for thinking that perhaps none of them are true in the sense in which they are thus meant. But whether these reasons for denying the truth of aesthetic judgements, except as statements of feeling, are sound or no, they do not apply to moral judgements. Mr. Ayer at least would not pretend to show that moral judgements are false. It was just because his general theory would not allow him to hold any opinion about their truth or falsehood as regards independent facts that he was attracted by the view that they only asserted a state of mind, and when he found that untenable was driven to assert

[1] *Language, Truth and Logic*, pp. 156–7.

that they assert nothing. The steps of my argument, then, should be to show:

(1) That moral judgements, as the word 'judgment' implies, assert something.

(2) That what they assert is not the existence of a feeling in myself or others, but, as they profess, a fact which is not a feeling.

(3) That once granted moral judgements do assert such a fact, there are no more valid reasons for doubting the possibility of their truth than that of other types of judgement, the motive for doing so being not any consideration of their own nature, but the desire to support a peculiar view of truth. And, in particular, we should try to show that certain arguments against the truth of any judgement which asserts beauty to belong to things independently of any feelings about them do not apply to moral judgements.

The first point, then, is that moral judgements assert something.

Mr. Ayer says:[1]

'If I say to someone "you acted wrongly in taking[2] that money" I am not stating anything more than if I had simply said, "you took that money." In adding that this action is wrong I am not making any further statement about it. I am simply evincing my moral disapproval of it. It is as if I had said "you took that money" in a peculiar tone of horror, or written it with some special exclamation marks. The tone or the exclamation marks adds nothing to the literal meaning of the sentence. It merely serves to show that the expression of it is attended by certain feelings in the speaker. If now I generalize my previous statement and say "Taking money is (in certain circumstances) wrong," I produce a statement which has no factual meaning, that is, expresses no proposition which can be true or false. It

[1] Ibid., p. 158.
[2] He says 'stealing'. I have substituted 'taking' as he is clearly not entitled to a dyslogistic word.

is as if I had written "Taking money!!" with two notes of exclamation to show, by a suitable convention, that a special sort of moral disapproval is the feeling which is being expressed.'

But let us take Mr. Ayer's language in this passage seriously. He says that if I say 'you acted wrongly in taking that money' instead of saying 'you took that money', the only difference (which he will not allow to be a difference of meaning) is that I *evince* moral disapproval, and, again, he says that the sentence 'stealing money is wrong' *shows* 'by a *suitable convention*[1] that a special sort of moral disapproval is the feeling which is being expressed'. But the evincing a feeling, or showing to others that I have a feeling, may be a voluntary act.[2] And when I 'adopt a suitable convention' for doing so, it certainly is. I clearly may tell or show a man, or evince to a man, that I feel disgust at what he is doing, though in fact I do not feel any, and he may believe me and alter his conduct in consequence. Evidently Mr. Ayer does not really think that to say 'you ought not to take this money' is a mere involuntary symptom of disgust, as sweating may be of pain; it is a deliberate attempt to *show* or convince my audience of something by a *suitable verbal expression*, i.e. to *tell* them something, true or false. And what Mr. Ayer really, for all his protests, has said is that it tells them that I am feeling a certain disapproval or, as he says, that 'a special sort of disapproval *is* the feeling that is being expressed'. But unfortunately Mr. Ayer clearly recognizes that the two sentences, 'I feel a special sort of moral disapproval for stealing' and 'Men ought not to steal' cannot be substituted for one another, since he says that there is no contradiction in asserting that stealing is wrong and that I do not have any feeling of disapproval against it,[3] or, as I should prefer to put it, it is

---

[1] My italics throughout.
[2] As it is conventional in some nations to evince to your host that you have enjoyed his hospitality by simulating a belch.
[3] Moore, *Ethics*, iii and iv.

a perfectly intelligible question whether an act for which I feel moral disapproval is in fact one I ought not to do.

Just because Mr. Ayer had been convinced by Professor Moore on this point, he has to find some other account of what the statement 'stealing is wrong' means. And he only sees two alternatives. He must either admit that when we say 'taking such money is wrong' we mean (however mistakenly) that a man ought not to take such money, or he must resort to saying that we mean to assert nothing whatever, but are involuntarily symptomizing horror. It is hard to see how he can avoid the first course. For he grants that people do *think* that they have obligations, or, in his own Kantian language, 'Moral precepts *present themselves to some people as* categorical commands',[1] and 'they have for some people *the force of* inexorable commands', where he cannot be using the word 'command' literally, since moral judgements may apply to myself or to a third person or to past time. So when such people say they have a duty they in fact mean (however mistakenly) just what they say; yet Mr. Ayer argues that nevertheless the sentence they pronounce cannot mean what he allows they want it to mean. In the same way he says[2] that a scientific sentence may be a pseudo-proposition (i.e. unmeaning) to one person, but not to another, since on him it may have the effect of making him believe *its* truth[3] or at least assume its truth. But in that case what is 'it'? We cannot either assume or believe the truth of a sentence which means nothing. For instance, Mr. Ayer says the sentence '*p* is a law of nature' may give rise to 'a belief in a certain orderliness of nature'. Yet he apparently holds that such beliefs, like moral beliefs, owing to a mysterious 'rule which determines the literal significance of language', are incapable of being significantly expressed or stated to exist. I am at a loss about the nature of this rule or who issued it, or why it is called a rule rather than a fact. It can hardly be of the type

[1] *Language, Truth and Logic*, p. 169.   [2] Ibid., p. 20.   [3] Ibid., p. 84.

'*Ought* in English means much the same as *Sollen* in German' or '*Ought* means the opposite of *ought not*'. So I am driven to fear that it was issued by Mr. Ayer, and that it is precisely the type of 'rule' whose validity he is claiming to vindicate, such as '*Ought* means nothing', '*Law of nature* means nothing'. If, then, 'there are laws of nature (or obligations)' and 'there are no laws of nature (or obligations)' are both unmeaning, they are not contradictory. The whole view is based on the sheer dogma that no sentence can have meaning unless it is either a tautology or verifiable by sense-perception. I am not clear to which category sentences expressing the dogma should be assigned.

We are led to the curious conclusion that there are a large number of beliefs commonly held but incapable of being formulated in any sentence, and, by a strange coincidence, also a large number of sentences commonly supposed to formulate just those beliefs, but really incapable of meaning or asserting anything. It is a cruel law which debars these potential employers and potential employees from mutual accommodation. Again, if such sentences as 'There are laws of nature' or 'One ought to keep a promise' cannot mean what those who use them mean them to mean, namely, what Mr. Ayer admits they in fact believe, how did he come to know, or convey to us, what these beliefs are? He tells us men believe there are laws of nature and obligations, but 'there are laws of nature (and obligations)' is an unmeaning sentence. Perhaps he remembers that he once held these beliefs and that, when he held them, he 'evinced' the fact by certain unmeaning sentences which he then thought asserted what he believed. So he now conjectures that those who utter similar unmeaning sentences hold similar beliefs; and he hopes that when he tells us that 'some men believe they have obligations', although 'they have obligations' means nothing, we, too, shall recognize the meaningless sentence as a symptom of a belief which cannot be expressed.

But, as I said before, though we cannot sweat in order to prove that we are in pain, we can always utter these symptomatic noises and so 'by a *suitable* linguistic *convention*' induce others to believe *something*, either, for instance, that we have obligations or that we think we have. Of course, the fact is that when Mr. Ayer says such sentences as 'stealing is wrong' have no meaning, he does not mean by his statement what other people would mean by it, or understand him to mean by it. Indeed, he tells us that he means by it that the sentence 'stealing is wrong' 'cannot be translated into sentences which refer to sense-contents', or, in his other words, 'it cannot be indicated how the proposition expressed by the sentence could be empirically verified'. So that all he means when he says 'stealing is wrong means nothing' is that it does not mean that the obligation has any sensible qualities such as colour, smell, taste, sound, or shape. And this would be true of some sentences which, I suppose, he would admit to express genuine propositions, if only about the speaker's state of mind, such as 'I never understood that before' or 'unverifiable sentences are meaningless'. The view really implies, though Mr. Ayer would not admit it, that what a sentence means to assert is the possibility of obtaining sense-data which might verify or refute 'it'. But what then is 'it'? Not surely, unmeaning sounds, for they cannot be verified or refuted. 'It' must be the belief which the sentence means to assert and which another sentence may assert is verifiable in a certain way. If a belief, and therefore the sentence which expresses it, are about sensible things, then the sense-perception of those things might tend to refute or to verify that belief and sentence. But a belief cannot be that it is itself verifiable, and the same simple sentence cannot both assert what is believed and also how the belief can be verified. Yet surely the belief itself must be capable of being expressed and the sentence which expresses it must have a meaning. If a conjuror says, 'There is a mouse in that box, though by the time you open it it will have disappeared without traces', he may be lying, but he is not making unmeaning sounds or even evincing feelings, and some people may believe him. That the sentences usually called moral judgements are not mere ejaculations which would be incapable of truth or of contradiction and are not even merely statements about the speaker's own feelings, is, I think, satisfactorily shown by Hume.[1]

'When a man denominates another, his *enemy*, his *rival*, his *antagonist*, his *adversary*, he is understood to speak the language of self-love, and to express sentiments, peculiar to himself, and arising from his particular circumstances and situation. But when he bestows on any man the epithets of *vicious* or *odious* or *depraved*, he then speaks another language, and expresses sentiments, in which he expects all his audience are to concur with him. He must here, therefore, depart from his private and particular situation, and must choose a point of view, common to him with others; he must move some universal principle of the human frame, and touch a string to which all mankind have an accord and symphony. If he means, therefore, to express *that this man possesses qualities, whose tendency is pernicious to society*, he has chosen this common point of view, and has touched the principle of humanity, in which every man, in some degree, concurs.'

Hume plainly thinks that if I say X ought not to have taken that money from Z, I can be contradicted, and that not merely by saying 'I doubt if you really feel the disgust which such noises usually express', or even by saying 'Hurrah for X', but rather by saying, 'In taking that money from Z, X behaved in a beneficent way, and *therefore* in a way universally or generally agreeable to human contemplation.' Indeed, the suggestion that so-called moral judgements assert nothing is so palpably false that I wonder Mr. Ayer did not try rather to bring them under his theory as what he calls

[1] *Enquiry*, IX. i.

tautologies. At least one type of moral judgement, 'I ought to keep my promise', seems to be of the kind to which he should on his own theory give that name. It is indisputable that men use the expression 'I promise', and I do not see how, when they do so, it could be maintained that they are either lying or deceived. For, of course, to say 'you don't intend to keep your promise' is not to say 'you don't promise'. And other people understand what we mean when we promise, and often alter their behaviour in consequence. Yet it is hard to see what a promise is if it is not, as Hume said, 'binding oneself to the performance of an action'.[1] A man could not without self-contradiction make a promise while explaining that he was under no obligation to keep it. Possibly this is what Kant really *meant* when he said that to will universal promise-breaking involved a contradiction. If he did, we should have to suppose that by his phrase 'willing universal promise-breaking is contradictory' (a phrase I have never understood) he meant 'denying the obligation to keep a promise which you have made is contradictory'. Curiously enough, Hobbes seems to have held this view:[2]

'When a man hath abandoned, or granted away his Right, then is he said to be OBLIGED, or BOUND, not to hinder those, to whom such Right is granted, or abandoned, from the benefit of it: and that he *Ought*, and it is his DUTY, not to make voyd that voluntary act of his own: and that such hindrance is INJUSTICE, and INJURY, as being *sine jure*; the Right being before renounced, or transferred. So that *Injury*, or *Injustice*, in the controversies of the world, is somewhat like to that, which in the disputations of Scholers is called *Absurdity*. For as it is there called an Absurdity to contradict what one maintained in the Beginning; so in the world, it is called Injustice and Injury, voluntarily to undo that, which from the Beginning he hath voluntarily done.'

§ 2. To come now to my second point. If we agree with Hume that Mr. Ayer is wrong in saying that moral judge-

---

[1] *Treatise*, III. ii. 5.　　　　　[2] *Leviathan*, xiv.

ments assert nothing, we must agree with Mr. Ayer that Hume is wrong in saying that what they assert is the prevalence among mankind of a certain pleasure or distaste, arising from sympathy, in the contemplation of human dispositions and of the acts in which they issue.[1] Just as I think Hume satisfactorily refutes Mr. Ayer's view, so I think Mr. Ayer satisfactorily refutes this of Hume. Mr. Ayer says:

'We reject the subjectivist view that to call an action right, or a thing good, is to say that it is generally approved of, because it is not self-contradictory to assert [he might have added it is quite natural and usual to assert] that some actions which are generally approved of are not right, or that some things which are generally approved of are not good. And we reject the alternative subjectivist view that a man who asserts that a certain action is right, or that a certain thing is good, is saying that he himself approves of it, on the ground that a man who confessed that he sometimes approved of what was bad or wrong would not be contradicting himself.'[2]

In other words, it is as absurd to translate 'I ought not to steal' into 'Most men (or I) disapprove of stealing' as it would be to translate 'There are canals in Mars' into 'I (or most men) think there are'. Mr. Ayer then satisfactorily refutes Hume. And what is perhaps almost as interesting is that Hume himself is unable consistently and comfortably to maintain this position. His general view, no doubt, is that there is no such fact as obligation, but only general feelings of pleasure or uneasiness in the contemplation of felicific or pernicious dispositions and acts. He equates good and evil with pleasure and pain.[3] He denies that acts are really right or wrong.[4] 'The distinction of moral good and evil is founded on the pleasure or pain which results from the view of any sentiment or character.'[5] 'It is the nature and indeed the definition of

[1] Broad (*Five Types of Ethical Theory*, p. 115) points out that on this view moral judgements would be verifiable by questionnaires.
[2] *Language, Truth and Logic*, p. 153.   [3] *Treatise*, II. iii. 9.
[4] Ibid. III. i. 1.   [5] Ibid. III. ii. 8.

virtue, that it is a *quality of the mind agreeable to or approved by every one who considers or contemplates it.*[1] The only difference between parricide and the choking by a sapling of its parent tree lies in the different feelings with which we regard the two.[2] Such, I say, is Hume's general view, but he is too candid to stick to it. He continually, however inconsistently, insists that all who do not condemn acts done in the belief that they are pernicious and approve those done in the belief that they are beneficent are not only exceptional, but in fact wrong. Since benevolent acts and dispositions have in fact a tendency to promote felicity, they always *deserve* the approval of human beings, which they obtain from all those who have any 'rectitude of disposition'.[3] The rules of justice arise from the aversion to doing a *hardship* to another (as distinct from merely harming him).[4] A promise is described as a form of words by which 'a man binds himself to the performance of any action' and thereby 'subjects himself to the penalty of never being trusted again in case of failure'. At last,[5] Hume is constrained to face the question of what is meant by saying we 'ought' to be honest if we think it not the best policy. He 'confesses that if a man think this much requires an answer it would be a little difficult to find any which will to him appear satisfactory'. He discredits the holders of such 'pernicious' views by suggesting that their 'practice will be answerable to their speculation'. '*Ingenuous* natures' have 'an antipathy to *treachery* and roguery'. 'Consciousness of *integrity* . . . will be cultivated by every *honest* man who *feels the importance* of it.' Here Hume is trying to defend what he calls our 'interested obligation to virtue', and finds he can only do it by maintaining, against Hobbes, that we all have a disinterested (moral) liking to contemplate acts tending to the welfare of others, just as he thinks we have a disinterested (aesthetic) liking to contem-

---

[1] *Enquiry*, viii.   [2] *Treatise*, III. i. i.   [3] *Enquiry*, App. I.
[4] Ibid., App. III.   [5] Ibid. ix. 2.

plate *things* useful to them. Yet he can only make this a
plausible account of obligation by substituting for 'liking'
'approval', and by insisting that those in whom it does not
prevail are not merely abnormal, but base, villainous, depraved, rogues—language which would be silly if applied to
a taste for sherbet or Edgar Wallace. To say that honesty
will be cultivated by every honest man who feels the importance of it is either to say that if you like being honest you
like it, or that you ought to be honest. The whole argument
is only one of those, in Hume's own words, 'sufficient for
discourse, and serving all our purposes in company, in the
pulpit, on the theatre, and in the schools'.[1] Arguing against
the view that moral distinctions are artificial or arbitrary, he
says: 'Had nature made no such distinction, founded in the
original constitution of the mind, the words *honourable* and
shameful, *lovely* and *odious*, *noble* and *despicable*, had never
had place in any language; nor could politicians, had they
invented these terms, ever have been able to render them
intelligible, or make them convey any idea to the audience.'
He should have asked himself whether philosophers would
have been more successful had they invented the term
obligation.

Holding, as he does, that what we call obligation is merely
the liking for those acts whose felicific nature gives us a
sympathetic pleasure, he finds strange the fact that 'a convenient house and a virtuous character cause not the same
feeling of approbation, even though the source of our approbation be the same and flows from sympathy and an idea of
their utility. There is something very inexplicable in this
variation of our feelings.' I suggest the explanation that the
sources are in fact, as Hume would say, 'pretty different'.
He has in fact anticipated and applied to morals the modern
'Empathy' (*Einfühlung*) theory of aesthetics, which holds
that, when we call things beautiful, we have illicitly projected

[1] *Treatise*, III. iii. 3.

into them pleasurable feelings in activities of which we are capable, and which their shapes or movements suggest. So Hume thought that we call good those acts or characters which would give us pleasure in ourselves or our neighbours.

Adam Smith seems to be troubled at this inconsistency by which Hume, while asserting a moral judgement to be merely the statement that men have a feeling of a certain kind, also tries to justify this feeling by asserting that we are stating it to be a feeling aroused by the intended utility of the action, i.e. that we are stating some fact about the action or the agent. Accordingly Smith abandons the reference to utility. 'The idea of the utility of all qualities of this kind is plainly an afterthought, and not what first recommends them to our approbation.'[1] What, then, is it that so recommends them? He answers:

'To approve of the passions of another, as suitable to their objects, is the same thing as to observe that we entirely sympathize with them. . . . His own sentiments are the standards and measures by which he judges of mine. . . . In the suitableness or unsuitableness, in the proportion or disproportion which the affection *seems* to bear to the cause or object which excites it, consists the propriety or impropriety, the decency or ungracefulness of the consequent action.'[2]

That is to say, an action is *really* improper if it springs from a feeling which *seems* to me improper. This is Hume reduced to consistency. It is clearly intended to put moral approval into the same category with aesthetic approval. For it has been often and not unplausibly held that we approve works of art and scenes of nature when they express a feeling with which we sympathize or with which they succeed in making us sympathize. But no more than Hume can Smith be quite content with such moral subjectivity. To this account of 'the decency or ungracefulness of an action' he inconsequently appends a quite different account of its 'merits'. 'In the

---

[1] *Theory of the Moral Sentiments*, I. i. 4.   [2] Ibid. I. i. 3.

beneficial or hurtful nature of the effects which the affection aims at, or tends to produce, consists the *merit* or *demerit* of the action, the quality by which it is *entitled* to reward or *deserving* of punishment.'

So far, then, I have tried to maintain (1) that judgements about obligation *are* judgements; that is, they assert a fact and can be intelligibly contradicted. This, I think, Hume shows. And (2) that they do not assert anything about our own feelings or those of others, but a fact, namely an obligation, which though it may depend upon somebody having or being capable of some feeling, is not itself a feeling. And this, I think, Mr. Ayer shows.[1]

It now remains to ask whether there is reason to think that all judgements thus asserting obligations must be false because on reflection we see that what we took for obligation is in fact a feeling. The answer seems to be: there is no such reason apart from the *dogma* that no judgements are true, or that there is no reason to think them so, unless they either could be sensibly verified or merely 'state our intention to use language in a certain way'.

The chief *argument* that moral judgements must be untrue is derived from a false analogy drawn between them and aesthetic judgements, which are assumed to be untrue if intended to assert an objective beauty. But just as I think the view that so-called moral judgements are meant to state the feelings of those who make them or of others is false, so I think the view that on reflection we should see that consequently they are untrue, and that we must substitute for them judgements which do state the feelings of ourselves or others about actions is also false. And this latter false view, I believe, is closely connected with the venerable failure to distinguish moral and aesthetic experience.[2]

---

[1] See Ewing, 'Subjectivism and Naturalism in Ethics' (*Philosophy*, April 1944).
[2] See Ch. XVII below.

§ 3. The real motive for both views is confessedly the doubt whether there really are any obligations, and the implication is that when we use words asserting that there are we are meaning something false, or at least not known to be true, and for which no evidence from sense-experience or introspection can possibly be discovered.[1]

I take obligations to be relations of one rational being to others or perhaps to himself at a different time or to an animal; and surely there are relations, and perhaps qualities and things, perceptible neither to sense nor introspection. The relations of being 'necessarily connected' or 'implied', of being 'the square root of' or the 'grandfather of' or a 'species of' seem instances of this. Truth and verifiability are often called properties or relations of propositions or statements, though neither perceptible nor introspectible; nor can we perceive or introspect the 'things' called other people's minds. No 'logical words' such as 'must', 'or', 'nevertheless' are 'ostensibly definable'; what they mean is not perceptible. I know the reality of obligations and goodness with as much self-evidence as I know logical, geometrical, or causal necessitation, though, in any instance, whether I ought to do act X, or whether A is the cause of B may be dubious. I cannot doubt the obligation to keep promises or to spare unnecessary pain; I cannot doubt that the man who, believing he has a duty, tries to fulfil it to his own hindrance does a good act. It is less self-evident to me that there are other human beings I can affect than that, if there are, I have obligations to them. Were I (*per impossibile*) convinced that I really had no claims on my neighbours, nor they on me, I should have to conclude that they were not really, as they seem, beings like myself. Oblivion or self-deception about particular obligations to others is commonly due to lack of imagination, which enables us to assume that these others are 'quite different'. Such a defect may be alleviated by

[1] Cf. Ch. XVII, § 7.

any poetical or prose fiction which rises above the level of *rapportage*.[1]

§ 4. It may be urged that, since I am not infallible, my failure to doubt something is poor evidence of its truth. I agree that many beliefs it has never occurred to us to question may turn out false if we have accepted them uncritically or 'taken them for granted';[2] but if we have seriously tried to doubt them and found it clearly and distinctly impossible, we can at least have no better ground for certainty; we see their necessity. In my nursery days, say the 1880's, I accepted that it was wicked for women to smoke, and can well remember the illuminating experience of finding it not difficult to doubt; but one may try for a lifetime to doubt the obligation to pay one's debts and have no success.

§ 5. Some of those who defend the reality of both obligations and goodness have preferred to put goodness in the foreground as their favourite candidate.[3] Probably they thought that even if some people on first thoughts supposed it possible to doubt the reality of obligations, they would hardly question that a man who sacrifices life or happiness because he *thinks* he has a duty is really good. And, this being granted, they would probably argue that if his sacrifice is good, the belief which leads him to make it cannot be entirely illusion. To me the facts that we have duties, and that to do what we think a duty for that reason is good, are equally clear and distinct; but the latter presupposes the former.

[1] Cf. M. Arnold, *Sohrab and Rustum*, ll. 302–8:

> As some rich woman, on a winter's morn,
> Eyes through her silken curtains the poor drudge
> Who with numb blackened fingers makes her fire
>
> .   .   .   .
>
> And wonders how she lives and what the thoughts
> Of that poor drudge may be.

[2] Cook Wilson, *Statement and Inference*, § 54; Butler, *Sermon*, iii (on superstition).

[3] Kant, *Fundamental Principles of the Metaphysics of Morals*, i.

§ 6. We have now to consider a psychological doctrine which would indirectly imply either that there is nothing that could be called an obligation or that, if there is, its nature is strikingly different from what we generally supposed. This is psychological hedonism,[1] the theory that no human being is capable of any action except the one which, at the time, he thinks will produce for himself the greatest balance of pleasure or happiness upon the whole. If this were true all our acts would have the same motive, desire for happiness, and none would be distinguishable as better or more meritorious than any other, though some might be wiser and more successful. It has, however, been contended that we might still think we had duties and obligations which possibly might be real, and if on any occasion we thought the fulfilment of a duty, such as to try to keep a promise, would result in a balance of happiness to ourselves, we should necesarily fulfil it, but, if not, not. This contention involves that we can have duties and obligations, and believe we have, which it is impossible, and known to be impossible, to fulfil, so that no blame or remorse could attach to their default. It could also be contended that when a man thinks doing his duty will for that reason conduce to his happiness, this state of mind is really good.

To believe that it is our duty to do a particular action which we believe we cannot do, and for the default in which we can therefore incur no remorse or censure, seems impossible.[2] But since the theory of psychological hedonism is now generally abandoned, we can defer the discussion of this point to a more convenient place.[3] It is enough here to repeat briefly the well-known refutation of the main doctrine.

---

[1] ἡδονή = pleasure.
[2] I suggested in the last chapter that we may have duties of which we are unaware, which we can therefore only do by accident, and for whose default we are consequently not censurable. At present I call it impossible to *believe* something our duty which we believe it impossible for us to do. Cf. Ch. XII, §§ 5, 6.   [3] Chs. XI, XII.

§ 7. We have impulses or propensities such as hunger, affection, wrath, which 'terminate upon their object'.[1] They presuppose no reflection or calculation, though, when this has intervened, they may be judged conducive or detrimental to our happiness upon the whole, and they are often indulged when they have been judged imprudent. This could only have been overlooked in an 'Age of Reason', when it was supposed not only that every man had his price but also that he was always 'sitting down in a cool hour'. The theory must at least be emended to the form that men always necessarily do what at the moment they most desire,[2] whether this be to gratify an impulse, which apparently might be an impulse to do a duty, or to pursue their happiness upon the whole. This would be less glaringly false psychology, but equally inconsistent with moral choice and responsibility. Unless we had impulses we should have no means of gratifying a reflective desire for happiness upon the whole, even if it could arise. We should be like sick children asking 'What shall I do?' but without appetites or interests. Every day we do things we know to be imprudent, such as postponing an unpleasant task that must be done some time, which will grow harder the longer it is postponed and whose anticipation will poison the interval.

§ 8. I do not think the doctrine gains anything when for the word 'happiness' in the formula is substituted the phrase 'his' or 'my good'. It is said: 'The motive in any imputable [i.e. deliberate?] act for which the agent is conscious on reflection that he is answerable, is a desire for personal good. . . . It is superfluous to add *good to himself*; for anything conceived as good in such a way that the agent acts for the sake of it, must be conceived as *his own* good.'[3] And we read else-

---

[1] Butler, *Sermons*, Preface.
[2] See Ch. XII.
[3] T. H. Green, *Prolegomena to Ethics*, §§ 91, 92, and cf. §§ 128, 129, 138, 145, 146, 229, 232, 240.

where:[1] 'A man who, under a sense of duty acts for what he conceives to be good is acting from desire . . . a desire for his own good.'

§ 9. In all these passages if *his own good* is used in the usual sense in which we say 'a selfish man only thinks of *his own good*' then the doctrine is 'psychological hedonism'. But in fact the meaning given to it by these writers seems to shift from this to the sense of *good* in which we say 'a *good* man does not think only of his own good but shares his goods'. For we find it added that self-satisfaction of a moral being can only be secured if it is sought where it *ought* to be sought,[2] namely in a 'common good' and 'the only good in which there can be no competition of interests, the only good which is really common to all who may pursue it, is that which consists in the universal will to be good—in the settled disposition on each man's part to make the best and most of humanity in his own person and in the person of others'.[3] It is difficult to see how *I* can 'pursue' the *universal* will to be good. But at least it is clear that the word 'good' is being used in two senses, sometimes absolutely to denote an actual quality of states or activities, sometimes relatively (when preceded by a possessive or followed by 'for') to mean desirable or satisfying to somebody.[4] The argument appears to run as follows: 'A man can only do what he thinks will satisfy himself; nothing will really satisfy him but increasing or thinking he has increased or trying to increase (it is not clear which) the amount of goodness in the world; if he succeeds in doing this we call him good, and say he has willed as he ought.' This identifies moral goodness or the good *will* with the *knowledge* or correct opinion of what will satisfy

---

[1] Joseph, *Some Problems of Ethics*, p. 133. Cf. my British Academy (Herz) Lecture, 1937, *An Ambiguity of the Word 'Good'*.

[2] Green, *P. to E.*, §§ 171, 177.   [3] Ibid., § 244.

[4] Other meanings of 'good', such as useful for a particular purpose ('a good poison') or a fine example of its kind ('a good case of typhoid'), cause no misundertanding.

you, and Green, as possessing this goodness which is a form of knowledge, knows not only what will satisfy himself, but what will satisfy or be the good of every human being. He tells us it is the will or effort to produce goodness. What we ought to produce is the desire to produce what we ought (namely the desire to produce what we ought), and we can only do this if we think it will satisfy us most. The definition of our duty is circular, and our duty is one we may be unable to perform.

The ambiguity at the root of this fallacious argument has actually been recognized by one of its exponents: 'the good which every soul pursues is what would make a man's existence excellently suited to bring satisfaction to his desires', whereas 'the excellence we have in mind when we say that just man or a just life is good is moral excellence; this consists in acting from a sense of duty or from benevolence or gratitude'.[1] There is no more in common between moral excellence and what is excellently suited to satisfy desire than between being well and being well beaten.[2]

[1] Joseph, *Essays in Ancient and Modern Philosophy*, v.
[2] See Ch. I, § 14, above.

CRUDE MORAL THEORIES

A. EGOISTIC HEDONISM

§ 1. It is clear that both the writers last quoted as examples of psychological hedonism differed from its earlier and cruder defenders[1] by inconsistently combining with it the firmest conviction that there is a real difference between good and evil conduct, which is not a mere difference of more prudent calculation, and by a generous zeal for moral propaganda.

I think, therefore, that the most fundamental distinction between writers on conduct is between those who explicitly allow and those who deny that we all recognize a real difference between duty and desire. And whatever their other faults, this is explicitly allowed by writers, who may be called Moral Hedonists, who assert that it is our *duty* always to pursue our own greatest happiness upon the whole, though, even after deliberation, we may choose or decide rather to gratify some urgent impulse which is incompatible. They have at least seen that some actions are chosen or decided upon because they are thought duties, though perhaps not most desired, and others because they are desired though thought contrary to duty; they have at least allowed the possibility of remorse and censure. They believe we have a duty, though no conflicting obligations.

§ 2. If this theory were true, in all deliberate action our subjective duty would coincide with a strong desire, since all men desire happiness, though not necessarily with the strongest, since men sometimes more strongly desire to gratify an impulse even when rationally convinced that it will not conduce to their happiness upon the whole. A man's happiness upon the whole must mainly depend on the

---

[1] Such as Hobbes, *Leviathan*, vi: 'Whatsoever is the object of any man's appetite or desire, that is it which he for his part calleth good.'

satisfaction of the greatest number of his desires, future as well as present, in proportion to their strength and permanence. On this view, then, morality is the best policy; men would have no duties to their neighbours, and their neighbours would have no rights unless they were said to have the right not to be used in ways which would cause ultimate dissatisfaction to the agent. Every man would 'have a right to everything'. A man who thought he would so get most happiness would be doing his putative and subjective duty by treating others like stocks or stones, and would be liable to remorse and censure if he did not, even if he were disappointed in his calculations. It could not be replied that the best way for a man to get happiness is to do his duties, for that implies that he has other duties than to secure his happiness; and, since we do not always *think* that we shall be happiest by behaving honestly, bravely, and beneficently, it would be confusing the objective and subjective senses of duty. It would mean that though a man may think he will be happier if he does not sacrifice his health and friends and fortune to the welfare of mankind, and therefore has a subjective duty not to do so, he is mistaken, and therefore has an objective duty to do so. But since by such a sacrifice he would be failing in his subjective and putative duty and would therefore suffer from remorse and incur the censure of all who know his mind, the assertion that he would in fact always be happier in spite of his sacrifice has little to support it, especially as he might never know the success of his sacrifice. The best defence of the theory would be that, since few men are devoid of some sympathy, if we cannot keep our neighbours' suffering out of sight and mind it may be prudent to alleviate it when that is not too troublesome.[1] The grain of truth which alone gives any plausibility to the doctrine will be considered when we discuss the question of obligations to ourselves.[2]

[1] Hume, *Treatise*, bk. ii.   [2] Ch. X.

§ 3. A variant of what is essentially the same doctrine is that men's only duty is self-realization.[1] Since only rational beings, that is real selves, can have obligations, it must be meant that their duty is to realize their good capacities and, if these conflict, in proportion to their goodness. If, then, there is nothing better than conscientious action, to tell us that our duty is to realize ourselves is to tell us that our duty is to do our putative duty, which might sometimes be to improve our intellectual or aesthetic gifts and sometimes to serve tables. Probably the formula really means that our only duty is to make ourselves better, but this is confused with the doctrine just criticized, that we can do nothing unless we think it for our own advantage or good.[2] The only element of truth here, as I think, is that one of our obligations is to try to increase the amount of goodness in the world whether in our own character or in that of others.

§ 4. Finally, a school which agrees with the last mentioned that obligations are real, but differs in not maintaining that the only one is to pursue our own happiness or our own improvement, yet maintains that doing our duty is in fact always conducive to our happiness upon the whole,[3] so that if a man feels happy he can be sure he is good, and if he thinks others are happy must think they are good.

It is hard to see what grounds could be given for this belief. If the happiness promised is in the nature of a reward it must either be assured us by an omnipotent, just, and veracious being after our death or consist in the approval of our own conscience; and in either case it must be a reward for obeying our conscience, that is doing our putative duty. There could be no reward of either kind merely for doing what was in fact an objective duty, such as killing an intending murderer, if we did it by mistake or to get his money, or if we thought it wrong to kill intending murderers.

[1] Bradley, *Ethical Studies*, vii.　　[2] Green and Joseph, cited Ch. III, § 9.
[3] Plato, *Republic*; Butler, *Sermons*.

§ 5. As to the external or supernaturally effected reward, this is a hope whose theological grounds I am not competent to discuss. The argument for it on purely moral grounds is fallacious; it is to the effect that since we cannot perfectly achieve what we ought to attempt, namely the adjustment of happiness to merit, this must be brought about by some other agency.[1] But we certainly may feel bound to try to prolong a man's life without thinking he will or can live for ever.

§ 6. As to what may be called the natural reward of conscience, I do not find it true of myself that remorse for acts or omissions I thought wrong at the time, especially if I have now come to think them right or if the expected bad results did not follow, is always more painful and permanent than the pains I might have incurred by doing my putative duty. No doubt it is different; but memory is weak and placable; whereas some sources of happiness, such as our own health or the welfare of those we love, which may have been secured in ways we thought wrong, are always with us.[2]

The religious demand for another world to redress the unjust balance of happiness in this shows that in common esteem conscience is not a full reward for either good or bad conduct. Moreover, the approval of conscience is rather closely simulated by the satisfaction of successfully exercising or having exercised any arduous mental or physical activity,[3] however irrelevant to morality. To play a hard

---

[1] Kant, *Critique of Practical Reason*, translated by Abbott, § 3. In the *Critique of Pure Reason* (transl. Kemp Smith), B. 526, he even argues that, if there were no future reward, the 'moral law' could be no 'spring of action', and so far, he is a psychological hedonist. In later works he answers the above difficulty no longer by a future life but by an earthly Utopia. See *Idea for a Universal History from a Cosmopolitan Point of View* (1784), *The Relation of Theory to Practice in International Law* (1793), and *Perpetual Peace* (1795), all translated by Hastie in Kant's *Principles of Politics*.

[2] Most of the war-criminals at Nuremberg showed few symptoms of a worm that dieth not.

[3] Somewhat inaccurately named by Aristotle ἀνεμπόδιστοι ἐνέργειαι. *Eth. Nic.* 1153ᵃ 15, 1153ᵇ 10.

game, to climb a stiff gully, perhaps to drive a hard bargain, all give the glow of something done. Perhaps of all vices idleness is most unfortunate in having no such cloak; this at least was the feeling expressed by Browning;

> the sin I impute to each frustrate ghost
> Is the unlit lamp and the ungirt loin,
> Though the end in sight was a vice.[1]

But all merely sensuous vices, like gluttony, are in the same case.

It might be urged in reply that Pharisees do commonly seem happier than publicans; but this may be less because they have fulfilled more of their putative duties than because their moral obtuseness gives them so few, and fewer still which are much opposed to their interests, since it is easier to pay tithes than to throw up a good job. Their moral ignorance is their bliss.

No doubt we all think that if our consciences were burdened with wanton crimes of extreme brutality we should be very miserable; but that is because we only describe thus crimes to which we think we should have been little tempted; those to which we are prone we are apt to call peccadilloes.

It is an odd consequence of this identification of putative duty with interest that a man's total balance of happiness would be unaffected by the greatest ignorance about his actual situation, about the consequences to himself or others of his actions, or by the greatest moral obliquity. Indeed we must conclude that this is not what has generally been meant by the doctrine that duty and interest coincide, especially for its first holders.[2]

---

[1] *The Statue and the Bust.*

[2] Plato seems to have agreed that virtue is knowledge, and whether this means knowledge of moral or of other facts makes no difference. Hume and Mill thought that the happiness of others is a chief means to our own; but it is secured by doing not what we think will benefit them but what really will, an objective not putative duty. More accurately, of course, what pleases us is never other peoples' pleasure, but, sometimes, the

§ 7. On the other hand, if the doctrine is taken to mean
that a man's happiness would be secured by doing his objective duties there can be no empirical evidence in its favour,
for nobody can know if himself or anyone else has ever done
this. So the judgement that the doing of objective duties
would bring happiness must be intuitive and *a priori*, either
that 'doing one's objective duty' and 'getting most happiness'
mean the same thing or that they logically imply one another.
I do not mean the same by the two expressions and do not
intuit the implication. If I meant the same there would
be no question to discuss. In fact I find that my putative
duty, the act which I think most likely to come near my
objective duty, is often incompatible with what I take to
be my interest; about my really objective duty I have no
information.

In no sense of duty can the reason why anything is our
duty be that if we do it because it already *is* our duty we shall
be happier.

It is noteworthy that if we believed that duty in any of
the three uses of the word coincided with interest we should
be relieved of one burdensome obligation to which most of
us obstinately adhere, though we do not commonly fulfil it:
that of trying to equate men's happiness with their desert.
For if happiness coincides with the doing of putative duty
the equation is already established since the man who does
that is, by supposition, happier; and if it always coincides
with objective duty, we cannot make it proportionate to
merit which consists in the doing of a putative duty because
it is so, and the two are seldom, if ever, identical.

Anyhow it would be interesting to know whether it is
because a man has done his putative duty, which he might

belief that they are or will be pleased, and this may be secured for a time
by doing what we think will please them, which is often a putative duty;
but the disappointment of finding that we were mistaken is great, and we
only try to console ourselves by reflecting that we meant well.

not have done had he been wise, or for doing his objective duty, which he might not if he had been more conscientious, that he is supposed to be happier.

§ 8. A formula of duty has recently had favour which I find difficult to understand as it seems either to be tautologous or to deny that there really are any duties; I cannot be sure which is the correct interpretation. It has been dogmatically stated in the words: 'A man's duty on a given occasion is the act which for him is both possible and necessary; the act which at the moment character and circumstance combine to make it inevitable, if he has a free will, that he should freely will to do.'[1] But if 'necessary' and 'inevitable' are used in the customary causal sense the addition of 'possible' is otiose; for nothing necessary is impossible. Must we then suppose that 'necessary' is used in the moral sense of 'obligatory'? The last part of the formula would then mean 'a man's duty is that which in the circumstances, his capacities being what they are, *is* his duty (and only a free rational being can have a duty)'. But a later passage in the same book[2] makes this moral and tautologous interpretation untenable: 'Doing your duty means doing (i.e. deciding by an act of free will) the only thing you can do (decide by an act of free will).' This makes it clear that in the first passage 'necessary' was used in the usual sense; that no acts are ever possible which are not believed to be acts of duty; that even if they were possible, they would not be free, and therefore could not be censurable. What it does not make clear to me is the sense in which an act that, given a certain character and situation, is inevitable and without alternative, can be freely decided upon. I cannot make sense of the matter.

§ 9. A view which I take to be the same as this, though not understanding them I cannot be sure, has been less hierophantically but not very convincingly argued for as

---

[1] Collingwood, *The New Leviathan*, p. 124.   [2] p. 220.

follows:[1] We cannot do anything unless we feel an impulse to do it rather than not. A duty is an act the thought of which arouses a sense of internal constraint which is different from inclination or instinct or considerations of prudence; it is an act I am ready to do in an inescapable way; I have no option but to do my duty. Yet though I think I must, I and others may expect I shall not. This is because the reflective will differs from the unreflective; the moral 'must' originates in reflection and judgement. What we ought to do is what we have felt bound to do while we adequately reflected and attended, and should again feel bound to do if we again adequately reflected and attended. Acts contrary to duty are those which we feel bound to do when we are not adequately reflecting.

In a later article[2] Dr. Falk says:

'To have a duty is to be internally required or commanded.' 'When we say X is (morally) obliged to do y, we are implying [or meaning?] that *in some manner* it is not open to X to do anything else. . . . This necessity is not merely physical [nor psychological?], for an agent can *think* himself obliged [but is he?] and yet not do what he ought.' The agent is *in some special way* impelled . . . or thinks he would be so impelled if he reflected.'

In this exposition six questions suggest themselves to me. *First*: on what have I reflected when I decide that in the situation I *ought* to do a given action? Surely on the various obligations, putative or known to be subjective, which the believed situation gives rise to. Had I merely reflected on the historical, psychological, and scientific data without considering obligations, my conclusion could only have been that such-or-such action would lead to such-and-such results

---

[1] Falk, 'Morals without Faith', in *Philosophy*, April 1944. The author means 'without religious faith', but his argument seems to imply 'without faith in the reality of obligations'. The passage above is a summary, not a quotation.

[2] *Philosophy*, July 1945. The italics are mine, as are the interpolations in square brackets.

affecting myself or others in such-and-such ways, or something of that kind; in short, my conclusion from non-moral premises could not have been moral.

Second: Is it true that when I am attending even to the fact of a duty I am necessitated to do the duty?[1] No doubt I believe that I 'must' in the sense of 'ought', but I am assured by introspection that I frequently do what at the moment I firmly believe I ought not; otherwise I should not blame myself.

Third: Is it always our duty to reflect and attend (whether to the facts of obligation or to other facts) so that further duties will become 'inescapably necessary acts'? If so, does this duty of reflection or attention become inescapably necessary only when we reflect and attend? and if so, what do we *then* attend to and reflect on unless it is the fact that we have some obligations?[2]

Fourth: In what 'special way' or manner are we impelled? I may think that if I reflected imaginatively on the pains of burning I should be more impelled to betray my friends instead, but that it would not be my duty.

Fifth: How can I require or command myself to do anything? And if I could, would there be any more reason for obedience than when I am required or commanded by another?

Sixth: If one of two partners thinks it their duty to pay £1,000 and the other thinks it is not, is either, on this view, wrong? If so, the definition of a duty as that which somebody 'is ready to do in an inescapable way' collapses. If not, how can either of them be right? Or are they both right or both wrong? In either case there could evidently be no real duties.

---

[1] Aristotle, *Nicomachean Ethics*, 1147ᵃ, puts forward a view of this kind but is evidently dissatisfied with it. He is clear that moral and immoral conduct (ἀρετή and κακία) have equal claims to be called free (ἑκούσιον); 1113ᵇ 12.

[2] Cf. Ch. XII, § 4.

To conclude, I think that an ambiguous use of words like 'must' and 'necessary', sometimes in the moral and sometimes in the customary causal sense, here conceals the view that there are no real obligations (recognition or conviction of which might be a ground for action), but only compelling impulses in our own minds, impulses which are not aroused by the belief that we are in fact morally obliged.[1] I fancy the 'reflection' referred to means attending to something, namely that we ought to do X, and not attending to something else, namely that it would be painful. And we ought so to attend and not attend.

B. HEDONISTIC UTILITARIANISM

§ 10. Many of those who held that a man's only duty is to pursue his own happiness asserted, as the ground of this duty, that happiness is the only good, with the implication that nothing but the capacity to produce something good involves any obligation. Some of them[2] came to see that if my happiness is good, any other man's must be so too; and consequently they substituted for the Egoistic Hedonism the Altruistic, better known as Utilitarianism, which holds that our only duty is beneficence, to increase the amount of happiness in the world. They did not generally recognize that, if happiness is the only good thing, there could be no goodness in an action done because it was believed, perhaps falsely, to be conducive to happiness, that is to say in what they regarded as the only kind of moral or conscientious action. They could not call a man good for *trying* to increase happiness even at his own expense.

[1] Cf. Hume, *Treatise*, 'Morality is more properly felt than judged of', III. I. i. I think something of the same kind is meant by Alexander in *Beauty and Other Forms of Value*, p. 251: '*Ought* is not the prescription set to the natural passions by some supposed non-natural element in our nature, not even by reason, but is the arrangement or order established among them by another natural passion.' The recognition of obligation is no passion, but I do not know why it should be supposed 'non-natural'.

[2] e.g. Sidgwick, *Methods of Ethics*.

Some strangely tried to combine the two theories of egoism and utilitarianism either in more or less confusion[1] or on the ground that our own good or happiness *depended* on that of others.[2] In this they fall under the criticism already passed[3] on all who identify duty with interest: they were not clear whether it was doing our objective duty, that is (as they thought) achieving the happiness of others, however accidentally, which would make us happy by sympathy, or doing our putative duty, that is (as they thought) trying, however mistakenly, to secure the happiness of others, which would make us happy by the approval of conscience.

§ 11. It was perhaps no accident that some of the most confused of these thinkers held the economic theory of *laissez-faire*. They thought that, though planning and regulation for general prosperity were futile, yet some secret intervention of a 'hidden hand'[4] shapes the selfish end of each of us to the greatest prosperity for the whole. So the doing of their putative duty (pursuing one's own happiness) and the happiness of the world (which they claimed to be their objective duty) would always coincide. The same thought recurs in 'Philosophies of History' which argue that since the 'divine tactic'[5] or the 'cunning of the Idea'[6] or 'the dialectic of matter'[7] inevitably shapes men's selfish and

---

[1] J. S. Mill, *Utilitarianism*.

[2] T. H. Green, *Prolegomena to Ethics*; see Ch. III, § 8, above, and cf. Hume, *Treatise*.   [3] §§ 4–7, above.

[4] The phrase 'invisible hand' is due to Adam Smith, *Wealth of Nations*, I. ii.   [5] Burke, *Appeal to Old Whigs*.

[6] Hegel, *Philosophy of Right*, trans. Knox.

[7] Engels, *Socialism, Utopian and Scientific*; and Marx, *La misère de la philosophie* (preface to German edition). The genealogy of this idea is instructive. Cf. Psalms lxxvi. 10, 'The fierceness of men shall turn to thy praise'; Mandeville, *The Fable of the Bees: Private Vices Public Benefits*; Kant, *Universal History from a Cosmopolitan Point of View*, 'Thank God for our vices'. Butler in the *Dissertation on Virtue* suggests a different view, that just acts may in fact always increase general happiness, though God for mysterious reasons has hidden this true ground of their obligatoriness from our conscience. Ruskin seems to agree (*Unto this Last*, ii).

mistaken ends in the interest of what is good, we can be sure, in spite of conscience, that it is always our duty to co-operate with 'the course of the word': what comes about is a sure criterion of duty, but unfortunately only after the event. As Schiller said, the verdict of history is the judgement of God.

§ 12. When utilitarianism is not contaminated by the relics of egoism it has always seemed to me the most plausible and, if I may so speak, the most nearly true of false ethical theories. It recognizes an obligation; it recognizes that this is distinct from self-interest; and the obligation it recognizes is a very important one; its error is to recognize only one. A utilitarian, if he lived up to his theory by always doing his putative duty, would perhaps perform more of his subjective duties than most of us actually do who hold a truer theory; possibly more even than a man who *lived up to* a theory recognizing any *one* other type of obligation.

Suppose a utilitarian and myself both always to have complete knowledge of our situations, of our capacities, and of the consequences of our possible actions. If he always did what, on his principle, he thought the situations demanded, namely to promote the maximum of general happiness, he might well come nearer to always doing what the situations really demanded than I do, though I also recognize other obligations; for I may both err in assessing their comparative strength and may fail to fulfil what I believe the strongest. And again supposing a utilitarian and one who recognized no obligation but that of justice both always to have complete knowledge of their situations, of their capacities, and of the consequences of their possible actions, then if both always fulfilled the obligations they recognized, I think the utilitarian might well fulfil more of his objective duties. Both would be historically and scientifically omniscient and both mistaken in moral insight. Neither would ever admit conflicting obligations.

Utilitarianism, perhaps because of its initial identification of happiness with the only good, has seldom been given due credit for the insistence that what is good must be as good in one man *ceteris paribus* as in another, and that the preferential production of something good in oneself is not the promotion of *good* as such. Several objections, however, can be brought against the theory.

§ 13. (1) One criticism frequently brought against utilitarianism seems to me invalid. It is said that pleasures and pains cannot be measured or weighed like proteins or money and therefore cannot be compared, so that I can never tell whether I shall produce an overbalance of pleasure in this way or in that. I cannot weigh the pleasure of a starving man whom I feed on bread against my own in eating strawberries and say that his is twice as great as mine. Such an argument might seem hardly worth serious discussion had it not been used in defence of applying to conduct a theory of abstract economics: 'There is no scientific criterion which would enable us to compare or assess the relative importance of needs of different persons . . . illegitimate inter-personal comparison',[1] and 'There is no means of testing the magnitude of A's satisfaction as compared with B's'.[2]

§ 14. But this argument, though those who use it are not ready to admit so much, really should apply against any comparison of my own desires and needs. I cannot say that two glasses of beer will give me twice as much pleasure as one, and still less that hearing a concert will give me three times or half as much; yet I may know very well indeed which will give me *more*, and may act upon the knowledge, since the two things though not measurable are comparable. It is true that, not being measurable, they are less easy to

---

[1] Hayek, *Collectivist Economic Planning*, p. 25.
[2] Robbins, *Nature and Significance of Economic Science*, pp. 122–4. Cf. Jay, *The Socialist Case*, ch. ii.

discriminate precisely, where the difference is not great,
than physical objects; I may be unable to say whether the
smell of roasting coffee or of bacon fried gives me the greater
pleasure (mixed with some pain of appetite) even at two
successive moments. It is no doubt often easier to read off
the luminosity of two very similar surfaces on a pointer
than to say which looks brighter, though in the end I have
to trust my eyes for the pointer. As we have admitted, the
mere existence of other minds is not demonstrable, still less
is the intensity of their desires. But if in self-regarding acts
I am sometimes prepared to spend my money in the belief
that I shall desire to-morrow's bread more than to-morrow's
jam, the utilitarian is justified, on his principles, in believing
that it is his duty to provide bread for the starving sooner
than jam for the well fed.

§ 15. In fact it would be no commendation of an ethical
theory if, on its showing, moral or even beneficent choice
were always clear, since in practice we know that it is not.
We often wonder if we can do more for the happiness, even
the immediate happiness, of our parents or of our children;
the former seem more in need of enjoyments, the latter have
a keener capacity but a quicker recovery from disappointment. Utilitarianism has no need to stake its case on the
possibility of an accurate 'hedonistic (or agathistic[1]) calculus'.
We have a well-founded belief that starvation hurts most
people more than a shortage of grape-fruit, and no *knowledge how much* more it will hurt even ourselves to-morrow;
and it is on such beliefs that we have to act; we can never
know either our objective duty or our objective long-run
interest.

§ 16. (2) The second objection to the utilitarians is serious
and indeed fatal. They make no room for justice. Most of
them really admitted this when they found it hard on their
principle to allow for the admitted obligation to distribute

---

[1] See § 19.

happiness 'fairly', that is either equally or in proportion to desert. This led them to qualify their definition of duty as 'promoting the greatest amount of happiness', by adding 'of the greatest number',[1] and to emphasize this by the proviso 'every one to count for one and no more'. They can hardly have meant by this merely that it did not matter to whom I gave the happiness so long as I produced the most possible, for this they had already implied. They must at least have meant that if I could produce the same amount either in equal shares or in unequal I ought to prefer the former; and this means that I ought to be just as well as generous. The other demand of justice, that we should take account of past merit in our distribution, I think they would have denied, or rather explained away by the argument that to reward beneficence was to encourage such behaviour by example, and therefore a likely way to increase the total of happiness.[2]

§ 17. (3) A third criticism, incurred by some utilitarians[3] in the attempt to accommodate their theory to our moral judgements, was that of inconsistency in considering differences of quality or kind, as well as of amount, among pleasures when determining what we ought to do. It seems clear that people do not feel the same obligation to endow the art of cookery or pot-boiling as that of poetry or music, and this not because they are convinced that the one causes keener and more constant pleasure to a greater number than the other. Yet the recognition of a stronger obligation to promote 'higher' or 'better' pleasures implies that we think something good, say musical or poetic experience, not merely in proportion to its general pleasantness but by its own nature. The attempt to unite this 'qualification of pleasures' with hedonistic utilitarianism is like saying 'I

[1] 'The *greatest Happiness* for the greatest Numbers', Hutcheson, *Enquiry into the Original of Our Ideas of Beauty and Virtue*, II. iii. 8.
[2] See Ch. V.
[3] e.g. J. S. Mill. Bentham more consistently held that 'the pleasure of push-pin is as good as the pleasure of poetry'.

care about nothing but money, but I would not come by it dishonestly'. The fundamental fact is that we do not think some pleasures, such as that of cruelty, good at all.[1]

§ 18. (4) Though the inconsistency of modifying their theory in these two ways seems to have escaped the notice of most utilitarians, they could not help seeing that they were bound to meet a fourth criticism by giving some account of the universal belief that we have obligations to keep our promises. It is obvious that the payment of money to a rich creditor may not immediately result in so much satisfaction as the keeping of it by a poor debtor or the giving of it to a useful charity,[2] and that yet it may, under most circumstances, be judged a duty and always an obligation. The argument of utilitarians to explain this has usually been as follows: It is true that a particular instance of justice may not directly increase the sum of human happiness but quite the contrary, and yet we often approve such an instance. This is because the *general* practice of such good faith, with the consequent possibility of credit and contract, is supremely conducive to happiness, and therefore so far as any violation of a bargain impairs this confidence, it is, indirectly and in the long run, pernicious.

Such an attempt to bring promise-keeping under the utilitarian formula breaks down because it only applies where the promise and its performance or neglect would be public and therefore serve as an example to others.[3]

Suppose that two explorers in the Arctic have only enough food to keep one alive till he can reach the base, and one offers to die if the other will promise to educate his children. No other person can know that such a promise was made, and the breaking or keeping of it cannot influence the future

[1] See Ch. VIII.

[2] Hume, *Treatise of Human Nature*, Bk. III, ii. 1.

[3] But see Ch. IX, § 13, and cf. the article by Mr. Mabbott in *Mind*, April 1939, pp. 155–7, where he shows that the reply to this 'indirect utilitarian' argument is 'keep it dark'.

keeping of promises. On the utilitarian theory, then, it is the duty of the returned traveller to act precisely as he ought to have acted if no bargain had been made: to consider how he can spend his money most expediently for the happiness of mankind, and, if he thinks his own child is a genius, to spend it upon him.

§ 19. Or, to take a different kind of justice, the utilitarian must hold that we are justified in inflicting pain always and only in order to prevent worse pain or bring about greater happiness. This, then, is all we need consider in so-called punishment, which must be purely preventive.[1] But if some kind of very cruel crime becomes common, and none of the criminals can be caught, it might be highly expedient, as an example, to hang an innocent man, if a charge against him could be so framed that he were universally thought guilty; indeed this would only fail to be an ideal instance of utilitarian 'punishment' because the victim himself would not have been so likely as a real felon to commit such a crime in the future; in all other respects it would be perfectly deterrent and therefore felicific.[2]

In short, utilitarianism has forgotten rights; it allows no right to a man because he is innocent or because he has worked hard or has been promised or injured, or because he stands in any other special relation to us. It thinks only of duties or rather of a single duty, to dump happiness wherever we most conveniently can. If it speaks of rights at all it could only say all men have one and the same right, namely that all men should try to increase the total happiness. And this is a manifest misuse of language.

C. AGATHISTIC[3] UTILITARIANISM

§ 20. In the hope of escaping some of these difficulties, especially the fact that some pleasures are judged better than others as well as greater,[4] utilitarianism has been modified

---

[1] Ch. V.   [2] See next chapter.   [3] ἀγαθὸν = good.   [4] See § 17 above.

by the admission that there are other good states or activities besides pleasure and that our sole duty is to do the 'optimific' act, to produce the best results we can.[1] This, for brevity, I shall call the obligation of *improvement* as distinct from the hedonistic one of beneficence. This modification of hedonistic utilitarianism corresponds to that already criticized, of egoistic hedonism, into 'self-realization'.[2]

The usual list of good things offered, though it does not necessarily claim to be exhaustive, is: Happiness or Pleasure, Affection, Aesthetic experience, and Knowledge.[3] This version has not the same attractive simplicity as the hedonistic variety of utilitarianism, since it allows a diversity of goods between which we may have to choose, whether, for instance, on a given occasion we ought to aim at increasing knowledge or happiness. But this very lack of tidiness brings it nearer truth, since it is clear that we do have to make such decisions and sometimes remain doubtful of the right one. It was a wise caution of Bacon to philosophers, 'Many things in the world are heterogeneous on which the human mind tries to force uniformity.'[4]

§ 21. But by allowing good things other than the happiness which all men desire the theory has raised for itself a new problem. Among good things one, perhaps the best of all, is surely an act done by a man to his own hindrance because he believes it to be his duty. This has been expressed in arresting language by the sayings that 'the only unconditionally good thing is the good will',[5] that 'the moral law within and the starry heaven above give us the greatest sense of sublimity',[6] and that 'justice is more admirable than the

---

[1] e.g. Rashdall, *Theory of Good and Evil*, and Moore, *Principia Ethica* and *Ethics*.

[2] Ch. IV, § 3.　　　　　　　　　　　[3] See Chs. VII, VIII.

[4] *Novum Organon*, xlv, and cf. my IV, § 14.

[5] Kant, *Fundamental Principles of the Metaphysic of Morals*, trans. Abbot.

[6] Kant, *Critique of Practical Reason* (conclusion).

morning or the evening star'.[1] But such goodness is not the *result* of an action, expectation of which *makes* us think it obligatory, it is in the nature itself of any action which is done because it is *already* thought a duty, whether on account of its expected results or for some other reason. Acts, then, which result in the best possible consequences have been called *optimific* or 'best-producing', and those whose intrinsic goodness combined with their good consequences together constitute the best possible whole have been called *optimizing* or 'best-rendering'. If, then, with the agathistic utilitarians we thought it always a man's objective duty to do the really optimific act, we should have to admit, what they did not always recognize, that if such an act were done from bad or indifferent motives, it might not be so optimizing as the doing of a putative duty, though, owing to ignorance, this was the reverse of optimific. Indeed, if we could accept the view that a conscientious act is always *incomparably* better than any amount of other goods,[2] we should have to conclude that the doing of any putative duty is always optimizing and consequently that optimization cannot be the ground of obligation. For what has to be emphasized at the cost of repetition is that the goodness of doing an act because it is thought a duty cannot be the reason for its being thought a duty. It might be thought a duty because it was thought optimific, and whether this belief were true or false, the doing of it for that reason might be optimizing. But any form of utilitarianism is committed to finding the ground of obligation wholly subsequent to the action, in the preponderance of good *results*.

§ 22. The objection, then, which we found fatal to hedonistic utilitarianism is equally fatal to the agathistic emendation;

---

[1] Aristotle, *Nicomachean Ethics*, 1129ᵇ 28, trans. Ross, and cf. Wordsworth, *Ode to Duty*. For Aristotle justice covers all our obligations to others: ἀλλότριον ἀγαθὸν δοκεῖ εἶναι ἡ δικαιοσύνη μόνη τῶν ἀρετῶν, ὅτι πρὸς ἕτερόν ἐστιν (1030ᵃ 3).

[2] Ross, *The Right and the Good*, vi; but cf. Ch. VII, § 1, below.

neither gives any account of promise-keeping or of other justice. The accidental acquisition of £5 by a man who has been promised £5 is not necessarily good. Nobody except the promiser need be under any obligation to pay him £5; the payment by the promiser need not be optimific, and may not be optimizing if done from fear or favour; yet it may be thought a duty.

Some later agathistic utilitarians[1] have withdrawn from the position that the goodness which in their view is the ground of all obligation can always be found in the consequences of the act. They have also had to admit that what makes an act my duty cannot be the fact that if I do it because it *is* my duty it will be good. They have then entrenched themselves in the vaguer position that the goodness which is the alleged ground of obligation lies in some as yet unrealized rule or pattern of my own whole life or the life of some ideal community or of mankind, a rule to which my fulfilment of the obligation would conform. But surely there can only be an obligation to conform to a hypothetical rule, pattern, or ideal if it is a good one, and its goodness will partly depend upon its demanding for its realization the fulfilment of obligations; otherwise the position is that right action is mere self-consistency: *Pecca fortiter* or at least *Pecca constanter*. When 'drooling' during a committee meeting it has happened to me to make a blot in one corner of the pattern, and the pattern then demanded like blots elsewhere. But in conduct the blot may be an assault or a fib which fails to achieve my perhaps beneficent purpose unless it is followed by massacre or swindle on a systematic scale. An end that might conceivably justify one such action need not justify the systematic policy which would alone

[1] e.g. Joseph, *Problems in Ethics*, viii, and p. 48. I think Professor Paton held a similar theory in his *The Good Will*. In his recent *Can Reason be Practical?* (British Academy Hertz Lecture, 1946) I think he makes the possibility of universalizing an action coherently merely a criterion or perhaps a symptom of its rightness.

complete the pattern. In patterns there are no rights to be infringed.

Neither form of utilitarianism is a satisfactory formula for all our duties. We believe we have various kinds of obligations, for which we can discover no common ground, arising out of the various situations in which we think ourselves. When these putative obligations conflict we have to judge which of them is the strongest so as to constitute our putative duty. It is only for the neglect of putative duty that remorse arises, blame can be incurred, or punishment deserved.

V

PUNISHMENT AND REWARD

§ 1. WE saw in the last chapter that punishment and reward were serious difficulties for the utilitarians, since both depend upon merit acquired in the past and not wholly upon good results obtainable in the future. Have we a right or an obligation to inflict pain for the failure to fulfil a putative duty, and, if so, on what does this right or obligation rest, and how do we assess the due punishment?

The answer of hedonistic utilitarianism is clear: always and only when it will produce a greater quantity of pleasure in the world are we justified in inflicting pain, and then we are morally obliged to inflict it on anybody, guilty or innocent; bygones are bygones. Even the agathistic utilitarian must say either that it is no 'use' bleeding for spilt blood except to prevent more blood being spilt, or else that a bad man pained is necessarily better, whether in the way of repentance or not, than one happy. This fails to distinguish punishment from troublesome quarantine or compulsory vaccination on the one hand, and on the other from the irksome process of education; it is not what is generally meant by punishment. If punishment is purely preventive, by incarcerating or executing a probable disturber of the peace, or if it is purely exemplary and intimidating, by flogging or announcing that we have flogged an alleged nuisance, or if it is purely improving to the punished man by training and edification, then merit and guilt are irrelevant.[1]

§ 2. We have seen in the last chapter that the agathistic utilitarians, by recognizing good things other than pleasure, produced a theory more plausible, if less speciously tidy, than

---

[1] Cf. Brunetière, *Après le procès* (on the Dreyfus Affair), and cf. the remark of Caiaphas in the Gospel of St. John xi. 50: 'It is expedient that one man should die for the people.' Cf. also Ch. IV, § 19, above.

their hedonistic predecessors, and this is well exemplified in their view of punishment. They can consider an improvement in the wrongdoer's character, apart from its possible felicific consequences, as a good thing in itself to be weighed against, or if possible combined with, the useful example of penalty and the prevention of his noxious proclivities in the future should the improvement be incomplete. So they can combine intimidation and prevention with improvement so long as the felicific results of the first two and the intrinsic goodness of the last are together good enough to outweigh the badness of the penal pain. This would almost equate a prison to a quarantine hospital with facilities for education; to make the equation complete the hospital should be so notoriously uncomfortable as to make people careful of infection in future. It is no bad account of our policy in educating a child, for we try to make him both capable of useful service and also a better character, and we may even by praise and prizes advertise his example to others. But it still overlooks that reference to past guilt which makes us at least less careful to spare the rod to the guilty.

§ 3. The word 'retribution' has fallen into ill favour by being infected with ideas of vengeance. But the private vendetta is a crude substitute for justice when that impartial tribunal is wanting which civilized governments afford their citizens and which we aspire to provide for nations.[1] It is the essence of justice that no man should judge in his own cause; it is the mark of vengeance to extract a tooth for a tooth.

On the other hand, it is not clear to me that the natural indignation against cruelty and oppression which expresses itself in non-legal acts of punishment is bad.[2] There is such

[1] Locke, *Essay on Civil Government.*
[2] On the 14th of April 1945 there appeared in the daily press (e.g. *News Chronicle*) an account of the overrunning by the British Second Army of an S.S. concentration camp at Celle, near Hanover, where the surviving prisoners were in a loathsome state of filth, famine, and mutilation. The British medical officer ordered the burgomaster to bring citizens with

a thing as guilt, though perhaps less than used to be supposed when the extenuating circumstance of environment was underrated and that of neurosis uninvented. If good conduct merits reward, guilt would seem to deserve punishment, which may be indistinguishable from the forfeiture of common kindness; I at least am aware of having done so, and I do not merely mean that I might have been improved by it. The utilitarians of course drain all such words of their usual meaning and explain them by saying that it is useful to penalize, or pretend to penalize, those who are thought to have been bad examples and to reward, or pretend to reward, those who are thought to have been good, in order to encourage either themselves or the others. Since we insist that this is not the usual or proper meaning of desert, reward, punishment, or at least not the whole of it, it remains to ask what is.

§ 4. Does 'guilt' give us an obligation to inflict pain, or only a right to do so if it is for the benefit of other people and perhaps of the guilty party himself, though we might not have had the right if he were innocent? That it gives us the right I feel certain, but I am not sure that I should be obliged to pain a cruel man when there was no hope of reforming him and the punishment would have no deterrent effect upon himself or others.

An argument used against accepting a retributive as well as a utilitarian ground for legal punishment is that it is impossible to assess guilt. A man who has committed larceny or assault may have lived a better life on the whole than respectable citizens who have been harsh and oppressive in every social relation; we can only guess at the deserts even of those we know very well. It seems true that on purely

bath-tubs, hot water, soap, and themselves to wash the prisoners and to provide them with clean clothes, and then thoroughly to clean and disinfect the camp. I do not think the washing would have been worse done by our men, but the whole affair would have been less good.

retributive grounds we should not risk assigning punishments by the hit-or-miss of criminal procedure. Yet our emphasis on the proof of guilt, our subsequent admission of extenuating circumstances and of past record, as well as the customary judicial reproof, imply that ill-desert is a necessary condition, though not the complete justification of legal punishment. Though we do not know the man's other faults or merits, the fact that in some particular he has fallen below the common standards of duty is a probable justification for using him as a means to the welfare of others and for forcibly improving his conduct, and if possible his character, in the future.

That the *intention* of legal punishment is mainly preventive appears from two facts : (1) the penalty must be announced beforehand, since retrospective legislation would be for this purpose pointless and the absence of all rules simply stultifying; (2) the punishment must be known, either through being publicly administered or through being notified by exhibition or by communication to a literate public. On the other hand, the scrupulous demand for proof of guilt shows that the *justification* of this preventive measure is retributive. It is desired, at least, to inculcate the belief that the penalty is morally deserved, or it will not be supported by opinion.

It has, indeed, been held that legal punishment is pure retribution, that is to say deserved, yet deserved for doing something not morally wrong, namely breaking any promulgated rule applying to a community. It would not matter who made the rule or whether they made it on beneficent grounds or for their own convenience, if they had the power. If it were a stupid or cruel or selfish rule it might be a duty to break it, but it would also be a duty for officials to 'punish' and for any member of the community to aid them by confession or information. I cannot understand this rule-idolatry. No doubt *almost* any laws are better than none, and there is some obligation not publicly to disobey a fairly bad law if that would weaken respect for a fairly good system of laws. But I should not think even retrospective legislation against Jew-torture, nor indeed the lynching of a Jew-torturer, quite so morally 'objectionable'[1] as legislation enjoining Jew-torture or obedience to such legislation or the infliction of prescribed penalties for disobedience. Retribution divorced from moral desert is sheer terrorism.

§ 5. But a somewhat similar argument has been used against the whole principle of retribution.[2] It is said there is no way of making the punishment fit the crime, so that if a man deserves five lashes or five weeks, six is an injustice which we know not how to guard against. This argument, often used by utilitarians, is similar to one I have already mentioned as unfairly used against them.[3] If we cannot ascribe any mathematical proportion to our various pains or pleasures among themselves, nor to the strength of our obligations and temptations and the consequent guilt or merit, it is not to be expected that we could find a one-to-one equivalence between desert and penalty. Yet as we may generally know that two peaches give somewhat more pleasure than one or than two plums, and that to kill a man for his money is worse than to cheat him of it, we may have sufficient grounds for believing that imprisonment is a fitter punishment than the gallows for sheep-stealing. At any rate this argument would tell equally against the utilitarian view. It is impossible to know whether five or six months is just the period of imprisonment whose pain is slightly over-balanced by the felicific consequences to others or by the improvement of the criminal; and the infliction of more than enough for those purposes would be utilitarian sin.

§ 6. If we think a man humbled and broken in spirit because of his guilt is a less bad fact than one triumphant in

---

[1] Mabbott, in *Mind*, April 1939, and contrast Lamont, *Principles of Moral Judgement*, ii.
[2] Cf. Rashdall, *Theory of Good and Evil*, I. ix.   [3] Ch. IV, § 13.

his insolence, that may be partly because we think him more apt to future contrition. At any rate, punishment may be regarded as a sort of substitute for repentance, since adequate remorse, if we could be sure of it, would involve absolution, being itself the punishment that exactly fits the crime; and it is hard, either on a utilitarian or a retributive theory, to see any other justification for forgiveness, if that means remission of punishment. Our enemies, no doubt, we should always forgive in the sense of bearing no special grudge and exacting no severer retribution because it is ourselves that they have injured. To say that 'vengeance' belongs to God is to say that it should be not vengeance but impartial retribution, justified by knowledge of men's hearts.

§ 7. This point brings to our notice the curious parallel and contrast between punishment and reward. It has been held that we have a strong obligation to proportion happiness to desert. The utilitarian had to justify the infliction of any pain, but when benefits are conferred he has to justify the preference given to appropriate recipients. This, if he is hedonistic, he can only do on the ground that it encourages them, and especially others, to further felicific acts, and he should, therefore, insist that it must always be public; it is not punishment that prevents crime nor reward that encourages beneficent action, it is publicity—the belief, true or false, that such punishments or rewards have occurred and are likely to occur again. But this does not correspond to the ordinary man's feeling about repaying kindness or pensioning an old servant, for which he would often blush to find himself famous. Rewards only need publicity when they are honorary, consisting in honour, as penalties especially seek it when they are merely shameful; otherwise rewards look to the past, and, if the two kinds of desert were quite parallel, this would be an argument for retribution being the essence of punishment. But they are not: whereas punishment should never be by the injured, it seems highly decent that reward should be by one benefited. It is not recorded of the Deity that he said 'Reward is mine'.[1]

§ 8. It has already been suggested[2] that objective rights and duties are correlative as are also obligations and claims. What, then, would be the correlative of a duty to punish? On the hedonistic utilitarian view it would be the right of others to be protected from similar noxious acts in the future; on that of the agathistics there would also be the right of the guilty man to be reformed. On the view that guilt gives only a right to punish there might be a correlative duty in the criminal to submit, but on the view that it can occasion a duty it is an abuse of language to say he has a right to the penalty. Yet it seems we should have to say this, or abandon either the obligation to sheer retribution or the doctrine of correlatives.[3]

I am inclined to say, then, that guilt, in proportion to its greatness, diminishes a man's claim not to be hurt. Consequently we have a stronger obligation to hurt him for his own or other people's benefit or improvement than if he were innocent. The others may have a right to such benefit, and he may have a right to such improvement, though he may not desire it.

[1] But cf. Ch. IX, § 9.   [2] Ch. II.
[3] On the whole question see Ewing, *Punishment*; Bradley, *Ethical Studies* and *International Journal of Ethics*, 1894; Rashdall, *Theory of Good and Evil*, I. ix.

VI

NATURAL RIGHTS[1]

§ 1. HITHERTO we have said that obligations and duties arise out of some actual or believed situation;[2] that on the objective view they arise from the actual, on the subjective from the believed situation, and on the putative from the belief about what is morally required by the believed situation. We have also said that to objective obligations objective claims correspond and to objective duties objective rights. It is sometimes said that the word 'right' is used in two senses, in one of which it merely implies, for instance, that a man who has a right to enter has no duty not to enter, and that a man who has no right to enter has a duty not to; in the other only is there implied a correlative duty of another person, as when we say that we have a right to be repaid we imply that somebody has a duty to repay us and when we have no right to be repaid we imply that nobody has that duty. But surely there is no difference. If a man has the right to enter everybody has the duty not to prevent him; if he has no right to enter, nobody has the duty not to prevent him. Both of the alleged different senses imply a correlative duty in some other person or persons. All this seems clearly applicable to such obligations as promise-keeping and the relief of signal distress, but less so to those, which have also been allowed, of general beneficence and improvement, the increase of happiness and good. There is, however, an ancient and respectable doctrine of the natural rights of men, implying that every human being as such has certain rights irrespective of his special relations to other people, so that it is not always plain on whom the correlative duties lie, though they must lie on some persons. This would be the converse of the utilitarian duty of general beneficence or

[1] Cf. Ch. XV.   [2] Ch. II.

improvement, in which it does not seem to matter who gets the benefit or improvement.

§ 2. Historically the doctrine seems to have arisen as a justifiable protest against the idea that all rights and duties were in some sense 'conventional', either imposed by authority or fabricated by agreement,[1] so that it would be absurd to ask whether the authority 'ought' to be obeyed or the agreement made or kept, or whether an individual as such could have rights in the absence of any authority or agreement. The vital point to be maintained was that all men have rights, whether they are recognized or not, for these rights are objective; other men may fail to recognize them either owing to scientific and historical ignorance, and then there are no corresponding subjective duties, or owing to moral obtuseness, and then there are no corresponding putative duties. The importance of the Rights of Man for political theory will be discussed later;[2] at present we must consider their relation to the various moral views already discussed.

§ 3. For the supporters of egoistic hedonism and self-realization there are no rights; so-called rights belong to the 'unreal world of claims and counter-claims'.[3] For the utilitarians, whose only duty was to increase the sum of happiness or goodness, the only right of each man, though it might be of no advantage to him, was that all others should so increase it. Yet, as we have seen, utilitarians had covertly to recognize the reality of individual rights by the just, if inconsistent, provisos 'of the greatest number', 'every one to count for one'.

The disrepute into which natural rights fell was due to the

---

[1] Hobbes, *Leviathan*; T. H. Green, *Political Obligation*, § 136.

[2] Ch. XV.

[3] Bosanquet, *Value and Destiny of the Individual*, v. In general, idealist theories are, of course, bound to deny reality to rights and obligations in any sense except that in which they allow it to personal minds and to the physical world, that is so far as coherently conceived in an act of thought, which they would hold impossible.

temerity of those who presumed to define and catalogue them as inalienable in Declarations of Independence and constitutional preambles. Such propaganda mistook claims for rights, whereas the former are objectively correlative with obligations, the latter with duties. The usual items in such propaganda were the 'rights' to life, liberty, and property, and the pursuit of happiness. One would have expected either a right to happiness absolutely or only one to the pursuit of property or liberty or life. As there cannot be a duty to do what cannot be done, so there cannot be a right to what cannot be had, and, taken literally, these assertions are as absurd as the paradox that in a state of nature every man has a right to everything.[1] If each man had a right to complete liberty of action, in a world not perfectly unselfish and sympathetic his right would certainly interfere with the like right of others. If by property is meant that to which a man has a right, to assert his right to it is tautology; if it means simply the power to monopolize something, then to protect one man in such power deprives every other of it, and the question 'to what property has each a right?' remains unanswered and indeed unasked. It is as fatuous to talk of the right to pursue happiness, if that means trying to be happy, as of the right to freedom of thought, since it is impossible to prevent either; but if it means the taking of overt action to secure happiness, which will probably conflict with its pursuit by others, it can and should be limited. It is only *claims*, then, that men have to life, liberty, property, and the pursuit of happiness, and when their claims conflict each has a claim to an equal share; the fundamental *right* of nature is to equality of treatment in like situations. If we ask: 'equality in what respect?' the answer seems to be, 'equal liberty, or equal power of doing what they choose uncoerced and unintimidated'; and among the things they will choose will be to pursue happiness, certainly for them-

[1] Hobbes, *Leviathan*, xiv.

selves and perhaps for others, and probably to acquire possessions and to preserve their lives. Alternatively it might be said that each has a claim to *all* the happiness, life, liberty, possessions, and improvement for him attainable, but that this claim is always overridden by the stronger claims of others to some share, leaving him a right only to equality of treatment in equal circumstances. This formula has the advantage of implying a claim not only that the division of freedom, and of the consequent advantages, should be equal but that the total dividend should be increased.[1]

§ 4. The proviso 'in like circumstances' when speaking of the *right* to equality has been necessary since a *claim* to equality of treatment may conflict with, and be overridden by, some other claim such as that to have a promise kept. Indeed it is a commonplace objection to the natural claim for equality that men are not equal in needs, capacities, or deserts, and that equal treatment should only be given to equals. It would not be equalization of benefit to give the same ration to an infant and a heavy worker, nor of improvement to give the same education to a genius and a dullard, and perhaps it would be wrong to give the same amenities to a rascal and a saint. Claims and obligations, rights and duties do depend upon the situation, but the presupposition of morality is that all men, and to a less degree animals, have some claims, a very relevant though general element in the situation being their rationality or sentience. There is nothing we can have any obligation to produce, to maintain, to change or to abolish except some state or activity of consciousness; everything else is a means to this. To every man, then, and every sentient creature with whom we come into contact, we may have some obligation of performance or forbearance, and they will consequently have some claim which it may be our duty to respect; we must not treat them 'without consideration' as we might

[1] Cf. Ch. IX, § 4, at end.

sticks or stones, use them for our convenience and then throw them on the fire. And the consideration they have an equal right to must be·equal or fair consideration. The claims of animals are fewer and in general less strong than those of men and our correlative obligations follow suit.

Allowance for need is merely the attempt to give equal satisfaction to different wants or to remedy inequalities arising from nature, accident, and social institutions. Allowance for desert may be either a different obligation competing with this or an attempt to compensate voluntary moral sacrifices, mental or physical, and so to restore equality of satisfactions. Allowance for capacity is sometimes the same as allowance for the special needs and interests of the patient, sometimes an attempt to equalize benefit for the rest of the population by the best use of those most serviceably gifted.[1]

§ 5. The formula that 'every man has the right to be equally considered' sounds even vaguer than that 'every one should count for one', but I take it to mean that each has some claims and that we must seriously ask ourselves what, in the situation arising from his character and relations, these may be. 'Equality of consideration' means impartiality, consideration only of morally relevant circumstances, the effort to discount private preferences and to treat the uncongenial and the stranger as we would approve of their treating us or one another; and this implies that where we see no moral ground for differentiation they should be treated alike. In this elucidation of the phrase we certainly have used only words (impartial, relevant, approve) which have in the context moral meanings, but it has been contended all along[2] that any attempt to define moral obligations in non-moral terms is the heterogeneous, or 'naturalistic', fallacy.[3]

[1] See a lucid article on 'Equality and Equity' in *Philosophy*, July 1946, by Professor Daiches Raphael, who gives interesting illustrations from government administration of rationing, education, demobilization, &c.
[2] Ch. I.
[3] Cf. Ch. VII, § 1.

§ 6. Yet it seems that in some circumstances the outcome of that 'consideration' to which each man has a right will be that a man has no further claims, as when he has forfeited all by utter cruelty and selfishness or when his life must be risked and even destroyed to save many others. But in the second case he certainly had claims, which we have weighed and been constrained to find outbalanced; our duty to him has been done in considering them and trying to devise some means by which he might be saved as well as the others; and this effort was all he had a right to. The hopeless criminal, on the other hand, may have to be eliminated[1] like noxious beasts or parasites; his claim is less than theirs, since, though their feelings must be less severe, he is guilty and they are innocent.

[1] ὅλως ἐξορίζειν, Aristotle, *Eth. Nic.*, 1180ᵃ10, apparently paraphrasing Plato, *Protagoras* 325 a.

VII

TYPES OF GOODS

§ 1. In opposition to utilitarians of either sect I have emphasized the obligations of justice, but in agreement with them I have admitted the obligation to increase good and also the obligation to increase happiness whether it is good, as they think, or not.[1] It is therefore necessary before attempting the classification of obligations to attempt that of good things. As has been already implied,[2] nothing seems good except states or activities of consciousness; and I find the most indisputable and eminent instance of goodness when a man does what he thinks his duty, though he strongly desires not to; and this may be called merit or moral goodness. It has even been suggested that this kind of goodness is so incomparably the best that the least quantity of it would outweigh the greatest of any other.[3] But this is to admit that the difference is not one of degree but of kind, so that what makes moral goodness thus incomparable to other goods would not be a greater amount of the goodness it shares with them, but something else which should be called by a different name. If no conceivable amount of the pleasure of eating could possibly be so pleasant as the least recognizable pleasure of hearing music, it would be misleading to call both without qualification pleasures.

Moreover, the contention does not accord with my experience. If in March 1944 the European war could have been ended by the selfish treachery of a convinced Nazi, I should have thought this on the whole better than its continuance by his conscientious refusal to save his skin. I should do my best to bribe him to betray his trust as the

[1] See next chapter.   [2] Ch. VI, § 4.
[3] Ross, *The Right and the Good*, pp. 152–4, but cf. Ross, *Foundations of Ethics*, pp. 283–4.

guard of a concentration camp, and should have thought this my duty.[1] Nor should I think the return of a small loan merely because it was my putative duty would be 'incomparably more good' than laying down one's life for one's friends out of sheer affection. I think the two kinds of good are comparable, as are two kinds of satisfaction. The comparability of the moral with other kinds of goodness would save those who speak of a 'holy will' (that is one which, having no contrary temptations, of its own necessary nature always acts conscientiously) from the paradox that such a will is not so good as one which resists temptations. Though no one of its acts may be so good as resistance, none would be so bad as yielding. And since all men do yield to temptations, the whole character of a 'holy will' must be immensely better than that of any man; the incapacity for either good or bad desert might be vastly better than the capacity for both. Those who maintain the incomparable superiority of moral goodness might seem to put a holy will somewhere between men and animals. The contrary belief may have been suggested by a confused consideration of two facts. The first is the obvious one that no authority or obligation can conceivably override my duty, which is simply my strongest present obligation. The other is that no 'good of mine', that is, no advantage of mine or good experience of mine can, by the mere fact that it is mine, have any over-balance in the scale of absolute goodness against the like 'good of somebody else'. It may be absolutely good that a person of a certain character in a certain situation should have a certain advantage, but his sheer self-identity cannot be the reason. When the word 'good' is used absolutely it has a different meaning from when it is used relatively ('good for me', 'my good') and the two meanings are no more comparable than colour and weight which may both be called 'light'.[2] The capacity to produce something good in the absolute sense is one ground

[1] See Ch. XIII, § 2.   [2] Cf. Ch. XI. iii.

of obligation; but the fact that even the absolute goodness I can produce might characterize my consciousness rather than that of another is not. Moral goodness, in the strict sense, I can produce only in myself, by doing my putative duty because it is such; but if I can produce mutual affection either between A and B, or between A and myself, and the former would be absolutely better though less 'good for me', my duty is clear. This is the ground of the so-called natural right to equality.[1]

If moral action, especially against strong temptation, is the eminently good thing, immoral action, especially with weak temptation, is the eminently worst. The amorality of animals is perhaps indifferent.[2]

§ 2. Besides moral goodness there is the ethical goodness of virtuous dispositions, which have been defined[3] as those useful or agreeable either to their possessor or to his neighbours, which the spectator has therefore a sympathetic pleasure in observing, though also perhaps some envious pain. This would somewhat offend customary language, since it would seem to cover a good memory, which is certainly useful, and to exclude sympathy with distant and incurable pain, which is neither useful nor agreeable. If we define virtuous dispositions as those which lead people to do impulsively and effectively what reflection would generally or often show to be obligatory we seem nearer the truth. Virtuous dispositions are those for which we feel an esteem somewhat like aesthetic appreciation and slightly more akin to moral approval, and the greatest of them is 'charity', the cheerfulness in giving that God is said to love. If we could imagine two worlds, precisely similar in all other respects,[4] but in one of which the inhabitants were mutually indifferent,

---

[1] Cf. Ch. VI, §§ 4, 5, and Ch. XV, § 4.
[2] Of course a man can never think it his duty to produce any amount of good by an act by which he would think it wrong to produce it.
[3] Hume, *Treatise of Human Nature*, III. iii. 1.
[4] This is the criterion suggested by Moore, *Principia Ethica*.

like the Cyclops, while in the other they delighted in society and abounded with sympathy for each other's joys and sorrows, we should unquestionably approve the latter, though if many of them were incurably unhappy the happiness of the whole would be less. Very good men have prayed for the devil. The writer of the Epistle to the Corinthians when he said that, though I give my body to be burned and my goods to feed the poor, yet if I lack charity,[1] I am but a tinkling cymbal, would seem to have prized this disposition above purely conscientious action, and Aristotle seems to agree.[2] If morality is the *supremely* good thing yet the *completely* good character would have also to include sociability. Christian theology, unlike the ancients and Spinoza, has maintained that God *nil humani alienum a se putat*, or, more authentically, that he forgets not a farthingsworth of sparrows,[3] and perhaps the doctrine of the Trinity is a protest against autarky. Certainly sympathy, though partly a gift of nature, is one we have an obligation to cultivate both in ourselves and others, and this must be because of its goodness; hedonistically it is a dangerous pledge to fortune.

The opposite of affection, hostility in its forms of envy, hatred, and malice, is bad; we are apt to think this even about animals. Sheer indifference between human beings, though common, seems bad.

§ 3. A third candidate, with strong claims, generally acknowledged, to the title of good is beauty. But beauty, regarded as a pattern, say of the ocean bottom or the backside of the moon, which may never be perceived, has no value;[4] the goodness is in the experience; and if that is purely aesthetic, unadulterated with desire or vanity or propaganda or edification, the question whether the object which occasions

---

[1] ἀγάπη, 1 Cor. xiii.
[2] οὐκ ἐστὶν ἀγαθὸς ὁ μὴ χαίρων ταῖς καλαῖς πράξεσιν. *Eth. Nic.* 1099ª17.
[3] St. Luke's Gospel xii. 6.
[4] But see Moore, *Principia Ethica*, § 50.

it is 'in itself' beautiful may be irrelevant or erroneous.[1] It seems clear that the pure aesthetic experience is not merely pleasant but good, since I feel an obligation to cultivate my capacity for it when I would rather be idle, and an obligation to facilitate its enjoyment by others rather than that of the best-sellers or the beer they may prefer.

It is noteworthy that the Greek word for 'beautiful'[2] was the word also used most precisely for 'good', since the word generally translated 'good' was also used to mean advantageous, desirable, or satisfying[3] as indeed is the English word 'good', especially when preceded by a possessive or followed by a dative. If God saw that his physical creation was good, it may have been the object of a pure aesthetic experience.

Total incapacity for any aesthetic experience in a human being must be called bad; what is called bad taste might seem to be worse, and if its cause is an admixture or substitution of vanity, desire, or irrational propaganda, this may be true.

§ 4. All pure affection and all pure aesthetic experience then are good. Another candidate for the title, popular but more disputable, is truth or knowledge. 'Ignoramus' is a common censure; but so it is to be a picker-up of unconsiderable titbits of information. Philosophy, or the love of wisdom, and science are esteemed, but the curiosity of the gossip is ridiculous. If knowledge as such were good I should think I ought to spend every idle moment in learning anything, say the number of freckles on my left hand, and in imparting it to any equally idle neighbour. The goodness ascribed to knowledge seems more appropriate to 'intelligent activity' or 'understanding' or 'reason': the apprehension of logical implications or causal connexions, the distinction of

---

[1] See Ch. III, §§ 1, 2, and Ch. XVII.

[2] καλόν, Aristotle, *Metaphysics*, 1072ᵃ27.

[3] e.g. Plato, *Republic*, 343 c, 359 c, and cf. Prichard (*Philosophy*, Jan. 1935), 'The meaning of ἀγαθόν.'

greater and less probabilities and of both from certainty, the discrimination of degrees of obligation, 'imaginative' insight into the minds of other men. I am not sure whether a true belief, accepted on mere authority, say about the evolution of our race or about the solar system, has any slight value. It is in much the same case as the unreasoned convictions of lunatics and drug-takers about ultimate truths. It has been held that since these are not distinguished by their holders from genuine knowledge and yet are nonsense, the value of knowledge is the value not of a conscious state or activity but of the relation of such an activity to something else. But the reason why they have no value is just that, true or false, they are uncriticized and unreasoned and therefore not the same activity as knowing. If a man really reasoned in his dreams he would not be dreaming that he reasoned. The convictions of a mystic or tuberculous patient, whether true or false, may have felicity-value, if such there be, but not rational value.

We are inclined to say the knowledge of 'important' facts is good, but when asked which are important we can only reply 'those worth knowing', not 'only those which are themselves good'. Knowledge by description seems generally more valuable than by acquaintance, though faith aspires to vanish into sight. The apprehension of some logical implications, as in the puzzles which fascinated 'Lewis Carroll', seems worthless except as an amusing gymnastic,[1] perhaps because they are purely formal.

As some knowledge seems good, some ignorance seems bad and some false opinion; but as some knowledge has no value, ignorance or false opinion about the same facts is not at all bad. False opinion seems generally worse than ignorance, except when, as we say, 'it is near the truth'. It is better to think the first Reform Act was probably in 1831 than to be quite ignorant of its date, because it is true that the date was

[1] Cf. Ch. IV, § 6.

a little over a hundred years ago. The worst ignorance is that of one's own ignorance, which is a serious kind of error, the taking for granted of something which one does not know.[1] But even this does not seem to be bad about 'unimportant' matters, otherwise playful deceptions as of an 'April fool' would be wrong. Most of our life we are taking things for granted.

§ 5. There are other mental dispositions which seem to have some degree of goodness: courage and patience; indifference or cheerfulness in danger, pain, and dullness; cheerfulness in general;[2] modesty; candour; tact; wit; even dexterity.

Temperance and determination, though they have more authoritative support, seem more questionable. I do not see any good in the disposition to do a middling[3] amount of everything, but only in one to refrain from *too* much or *too* little, which mean sometimes more or less than is prudent, sometimes more or less than is right. Determination or consistency in carrying out a policy[4] seems opposed to moderation, unless the policy is one of temperance; if the policy is immoral or mistaken it is called ruthlessness, obstinacy, or fanaticism. Under temperance would come chastity in the sense of a 'moderate' disposition to sexual desire and its direction to a 'proper' number of objects which might be one. This as a rule makes for the happiness of its possessor and of the neighbours, and has the same kind of quasi-aesthetic charm as grace, or humour, or an appearance of health. An excessive preoccupation of this kind seems prejudicial to intellectual, aesthetic, and humorous activities and is a strong temptation to fail in many duties. A complete absence of sexual desire would, I suppose, be called neither a vice nor a virtue; it would be like being born immune from influenza or with 'fatty intolerance'.

[1] Descartes held this to be immoral. *Meditations*, iv.
[2] Spinoza's *hilaritas*.   [3] Aristotle, *Eth. Nic.* 1106^{b}25.
[4] Paton, *The Good Will*.

If any of these dispositions are good we have obligations to cultivate them in ourselves or others so far as we know how, but the cultivation or actualization of any may have to be sacrificed on occasion to more pressing obligations. Virtues, such as courage, may be used for bad purposes; sometimes they lead us into temptation, as when the tactful, sympathetic man finds it difficult to tell unpleasant truths. Conscientious action alone, though like other good activities it may have bad results, can never lack the most eminent kind of goodness.

It would be trivial to enumerate the names indicating various shades of mental disposition which we esteem and feel some obligation to cultivate. Faith and hope might be varieties of cheerfulness, toleration of charity, humility a degree of modesty.

VIII

PLEASURE

§ 1. I HAVE reserved for a separate chapter the question whether pleasure as such is good. No candidate for the title has received more impressive testimonials both from utilitarians and from their critics,[1] but though testimonials are generally significant of something important, they are not always the best ground for election. The hedonistic utilitarians thought pleasure had no rivals; to the agathistics it was favourite for a place, but to me the odds are doubtful. The favourable opinion arose from the obligation generally recognized to increase happiness, combined with the utilitarian assumption that there can be no obligation except to produce good; it was given plausibility by what I take to be the fact[2] that the belief in the existence of something good, past, present, or future, always arouses some pleasure. But the question is as to the truth of the converse: do we always think the occurrence of pleasure good and of pain evil?

§ 2. An argument that we do so can be drawn from the universal recognition by theologians of a 'problem of pain'.[3] If God is good, they have asked, how can he permit what seems so evil? Their answer, of course, has been that all actual evils are the necessary conditions of a good that outweighs them, namely, free moral goodness. If there were not freedom to do wrong there would not be freedom to do right,[4] and if none of our fellow creatures were ignorant or stupid

---

[1] T. H. Green, *Prolegomena to Ethics*, § 368: 'No one, except under constraint of some extravagant theory, denies that pleasure is good.'

[2] See Ch. XI, §§ 4, 5.

[3] See C. S. Lewis, *The Problem of Pain.*

[4] Aristotle, *Eth. Nic.* 1114^{b}24. The contention that if on any occasion we choose to do what we think our duty we are free, but if we choose not to do it we are not (e.g. Collingwood, *New Leviathan*, 28. 81), is to me unmeaning.

or troubled or insecure, it is hard to see what our duties to them could be.[1] Here again the assumption is that if we often have a duty to increase happiness, happiness must be good, and the conclusion follows, that if there is to be the goodness of producing this good at the cost of some pain to ourselves, there must be the evil fact of pain both in others and in us. The argument would not account for the occurrence of such pain as is unknown to rational beings and consequently not a condition of their moral action, but it would make the possibility and existence of some pain compatible with a belief in a good creator.

§ 3. I do feel some obligation to increase happiness. Is this because of its intrinsic goodness? Of two worlds exactly alike in all else, should we more esteem the happier? To deny this might seem wanton paradox; yet it is also paradoxical to deny that there are bad pleasures. It might be said that the pleasure of indolence, though good so far as it goes, is outbalanced by the resulting loss of happiness to oneself or others. But this argument would not serve for the pleasures of malice and cruelty (which do seem to occur) or we should have to allow that a pleasure in falsely believing one was inflicting pain was an instance of pure goodness. As we have seen in considering punishment,[2] it is at least questionable whether the happiness of a very bad man is not an added evil; yet if his pain would be in itself bad, it seems hard to think that its combination with its moral badness could come nearer being good.

§ 4. All these considerations are against the verdict that pleasure as such is good and pain evil; they favour rather the view that the value of pleasure varies directly with the value of the states or activities which occasion it,[3] and the

[1] Hume, *Treatise of Human Nature*, III. ii. 2.
[2] Ch. V.
[3] Aristotle, *Eth. Nic.*, x. 1173^{b}10, somewhat inconsistently with the treatment in VII. xii–xiv, where pain is said to be evil and pleasure an activity and an end. These chapters may be by different authors.

disvalue of pain with their disvalue. The pleasures and pains of sympathy, then, would be alike good since sympathy is good, and the pleasures and pains of malice (according as it was gratified or thwarted) both bad. We could not say that sympathetic pain was any worse than sympathetic pleasure on the ground that it was occasioned by something bad, namely the pain we sympathized with, for that would beg the question that pain as such is worse than pleasure.

§ 5. But against this view I find an invincible conviction that some if not all *innocent* pleasures, which accompany states or activities in which no other goodness is apparent, are good. I am at least certain that I have some obligation to increase them, and some to diminish pains which are not occasioned by bad activities. If I were told that I could make mankind more comfortable, I should at least think I ought to ask how. And if I were told that it was by improving their health, their housing, or their diet, I should not lose interest on the ground that such sources of happiness were not good activities. If I were told that my behaviour was causing a great deal of unhappiness, I should think that was *prima facie* a reason for altering it; though the pain caused by my rudeness accompanies no bad activity in its victims. I dislike putting a trapped and mangled rabbit out of its misery; I should naturally say I did it because its pain was bad.

It might still be that my obligation to increase happiness, or some form of happiness, does not depend on its goodness, any more than my obligation to pay my debts depends on the goodness of my creditor's enrichment. But I find it hard to deny goodness to some pleasures not depending upon any activity of myself or other agents, and which do not seem to accompany any *good* activity of the patient.

§ 6. There is evidence that many people, not unqualified to judge, have thought the apparent enjoyment of a soaring

lark good, and presumably also that of a purring cat. Blake
thought that a caged robin put all heaven in a rage.

I remember once seeing a small boy on a perfect first
morning by the sea, leaping about in the surf and crying,
'Oh! I am so happy.' I do not know that he had done anything to deserve this ecstasy more than a thrush in a May
sunrise. It doubtless had some aesthetic elements, though
probably less pure than my own in looking at St. Paul's;
certainly it had some purely physical, and next to none
intellectual or moral or virtuous. But it seems hard to deny
that it was good, and I might have been willing, and perhaps thought it a duty, to sacrifice say a little finger or to do
a month's hard work to produce some crowded hours of
such glorious life. Yet, since I should not call the child
better for being so happy, as I should for behaving morally
or for being affectionate, it might be argued that what was
good was really my sympathetic and aesthetic experience of
his pleasure, by capacity for which I am a better man. I do
not think this would be true, though I must confess that if
the child had expressed his pleasure by raucous noises or
by playing on a mouth-organ, which seem natural symptoms
of childish pleasures, I might have been less moved.

§ 7. The case with happiness or pleasure in some ways
resembles that with knowledge, in others differs. The
goodness of either seems somehow to depend upon the nature
of its object or occasion, yet it is hard to say what the qualification of these must be to make the state or activity good.
Pain seems more obviously bad than pleasure is good, but
knowledge more plausibly good than either ignorance or
error is evil, and no knowledge seems positively bad as some
pleasure is. A state neither pleasant nor painful would be
called indifferent, but much ignorance as well as error is
bad. Perhaps the indifferent intermediate state here is that
of not having something in mind at a given time though one
is not ignorant of it.

It may be useful to forestall here a point to be discussed later:[1] if we decided that pleasure as such is good we should be committed, as the utilitarians saw, to the view that we had as much obligation to promote it in ourselves as in others. If, on the other hand, we take beneficence to be an obligation distinct from improvement, it might, like justice and promise-keeping, be one which is only towards others.

[1] Chs. IX, X.

TYPES OF OBLIGATION

§ 1. UTILITARIANS, starting from the assumption that our only duty was to produce good, found themselves forced to allow an obligation to distribute happiness, and other good things if they admitted any, 'to the greatest number, every one to count for one', that is to say as equally or fairly as possible; and they seldom faced the question whether a gross unfairness in distribution would be compensated by a slight increase in the total. They were thus inconsistently committed to the recognition of two types of obligation which might conflict, improvement and justice. They deserve credit for insisting that if our obligation to increase happiness is founded on its goodness we are as much bound to increase it in others as in ourselves, but they ought further to have concluded that, for the same reason, it would not matter how we distribute it, since what is good is as good in one man as another. To say that we should distribute it equally involves the obligation of distributive justice; that we should distribute it in accordance with merit involves that of retributive. Goodness, like God, is no respecter of persons; what is good is neither better nor worse for occurring here or there, in the future or the past. If pleasure is good, mine is as good as yours; if morality, yours is as good as mine; if deserved pleasures are good they are equally good, if equally deserved, in all of us.[1]

§ 2. If, however, as we have seen reason to suspect, pleasure and happiness as such are not good, we find by the reports of our own and other peoples' consciences at least three or four distinguishable types of obligation. There are

---

[1] Plato, *Laws* 732 a: οὔτε γὰρ ἑαυτὸν οὔτε τὰ ἑαυτοῦ χρὴ τόν γε μέγαν ἄνδρα ἐσόμενον στέργειν, ἀλλὰ τὰ δίκαια, ἐάν τε παρ' αὐτῷ ἐάν τε παρ' ἄλλῳ μᾶλλον πραττόμενα τυγχάνῃ.

the obligations of beneficence and improvement, grounded in my capacity or believed capacity to increase the amounts of pleasure and goodness in the world. And there is the obligation of justice, which may perhaps be subdivided into distributive and retributive, grounded in my owing or believing that I owe somebody something and in my capacity or believed capacity to pay. We shall have to discuss the claims of other alleged types of obligation. That there should be more than one, or even that there should be many, might disappoint our prejudice in favour of simplicity, but I should see no ground for surprise. Any definitive classification of obligations indeed is neither to be expected nor desired; it is mainly a linguistic question, dependent upon usage which fluctuates with time and company in its treatment of border-line or mixed cases; yet the discussion of what usage, by grouping similars together, will be most convenient, is not unimportant.

A. JUSTICE

A. DISTRIBUTIVE

§ 3. In the discussion of natural rights,[1] we concluded that the primary claim, though one often overridden by stronger ones, was to equality, equality of claims to life, liberty, and the means of happiness. The natural *right* of every man was to have his claims equally considered. Such equality naturally takes account of needs. To this claim corresponds an obligation to distribute benefits, improvements, and non-interference equally, an obligation which also of course may be overridden. It might be argued that this obligation is not to be distinguished from that of retributive justice or reward and penalty in proportion to merit, on the ground that when we are aware of no difference in merits we assume that they are either equal or as likely to

[1] Ch. VI, especially § 4.

vary one way as the other. But I am convinced, however obscure the contention, that I have an obligation to treat men with 'equal consideration', whether as an arbitrator, when I have nothing to lose, or as a benefactor when I arbitrate, as it were, between myself and others as well as between my beneficiaries. When satisfactions cannot be shared it seems better to toss up, or to say 'first come first served', than to distribute them, like kisses, by favour. This is clearly so when I am in a position of trust, say as a military officer or the captain of a ship. In other cases the decision may be hard, since those I am inclined to favour are often those to whom I may have a special obligation as children, parents, or an old friend. The author of the parable of the hired labourers seems to have preferred equality to desert.

§ 4. A puzzling apparent exception to our obligation to distribute both satisfactions and improvements equally in accordance with need is suggested by the observation that we feel a stronger obligation to benefit or improve one person greatly than to distribute any number of minute satisfactions or improvements among different people.[1] We take it for granted that we should be more bound to cure one man of blindness than to save any number the bother of spectacles, and, if we knew how, to convert a sadist to philanthropy rather than to make any number more polite. *De minimis non curat lex naturalis.* Obligations have a vanishing point. Even with the generally stricter obligations of retributive justice, as well as about those of beneficence and improvement, very inconsiderable debts seem negligible. Many people evidently think it worse to cheat one man of a pound than every shareholder in a railway of a fraction of a penny proportionate to his holding. This would make an added complexity for any 'hedonic calculus' and also for our account of equality and justice. If there were 'not much harm' in cheating a million shareholders each of one-

[1] Ross, *Foundations of Ethics*, pp. 69–72.

millionth of a pound, it is hard to say why there would be much in cheating a millionaire of one pound which I might greatly need.

In spite of difficulties I believe that men have not only the right to have their claims equally considered, but equal claims to benefit, improvement, and non-interference until some stronger claim to the contrary has been established: the burden of proof lies with those who desire inequality.

It is sometimes held that the obligation to distributive justice is a form of the obligation to improvement on the ground that equality is good. But equality is not a state or activity of consciousness, and it is not evident that equality of happiness, goodness, or freedom would have any value if it came about without human agency and if the possessors were unaware of their equality. It does not seem bad that animals are in many ways inferior to men. The obligation to beneficence seems prior to that of distributive justice, for we feel none to equalize happiness by merely penalizing the fortunate.[1]

B. RETRIBUTIVE

§ 5. Retributive justice looks to the past; its obligation is not to afford equal satisfactions or improvements but those which are in some way morally demanded by the patients' past.

i. *Moral Retribution*

In dealing with punishment[2] we concluded that moral guilt may give us the right to use a guilty party, for purposes of beneficence or improvement, in ways in which it would be wrong to use the innocent; on due consideration his claim to equality of treatment is forfeit. Moral goodness, on the other hand, gives us an obligation to reward its possessor with happiness in proportion to his excellence, and

[1] Cf. Ch. VI, § 4.   [2] Ch. V.

we feel some obligation to deserve our gifts from fortune. Both these kinds of retributive justice have been presented as obligations of improvement, on the grounds that, though pleasure by itself is indifferent, its combination with moral goodness is the best thing in the world,[1] and that for a bad man to be pained is at least less bad than for him to be happy. But if I heard that a sadistic murderer were also suffering from cancer I should not think the situation any better, but only perhaps if his pain were the pain of punishment and he knew this. Punishment, then, if it is ever a duty and not only a right, does not seem to fall among the obligations to produce states of affairs in themselves good, but has a reference to the past. I think the same is true, though less evidently, of reward. We are inclined to say that it would be good if the more honest farmers had better weather, though we should also say offhand that it would be good if everybody had better weather. I prefer, then, to class our obligation to distribute benefits in proportion to desert with justice rather than with improvement.

It does not seem that we have any obligation to distribute improvement in proportion to desert. On the contrary we should generally feel more bound to improve the worse man, on the ground that both the felicific and the agathizing consequences would probably be greater.[2]

The obligation to make happiness proportionate to goodness may easily conflict with the obligation to increase happiness. If I could know that two men were equally good and equally happy, and that I could make one happier but not both, I should feel an obligation to do so, though it would upset the proportion; I should certainly feel an obligation to increase the happiness of both, though the proportion would not be improved, and a disobligation to decrease the

---

[1] Kant, *Fundamental Principles of the Metaphysic of Morals.*
[2] Perhaps the opposite is suggested by 'To him that hath shall be given'.

happiness of both, though the proportion would be unimpaired. But I am pretty sure that I ought to do more for the happiness of a saint than of a sinner and that I must compare his happiness with that of other saints.

ii. *Debts*

§ 6. One of our most self-evident obligations is the keeping of promises. Its evidence is partly due to its definiteness; there is little doubt, as a rule, how far the obligation extends or to whom and from whom it is due. Other obligations, beneficence, improvement, equality of distribution, punishment, are mainly co-operative; we must all do our share in making the world better and happier, and more free, and in distributing betterment, well-being, and freedom fairly, each of us undertaking the work that lies nearest to his hand. But the keeping of bargains is a relation of one to one; we could only say 'I have made the world a little happier or better'; we can sometimes say 'I have completely kept my bargain'. Nobody else can, properly speaking, pay my debts, he can only give me wherewithal to pay them; but if somebody else educates my children or cures their sickness, that obligation is removed from me: it ceases to conflict with my other obligations.

We do not think ourselves absolved from a promise when the other party will get no satisfaction from its performance, for he may be dead or distant, but we should so think if we were sure that, could he know of its performance, it would give him no satisfaction; and we might think our obligation overridden if its fulfilment would be bad for him or for others or unexpectedly very bad for ourselves. If a man in a fit of rage or despair claimed the promised return of his weapon, with which I expected him to kill me or others or himself, I should not think I ought to give it him.[1] Such cases have been thought to show that this kind of justice

[1] Plato, *Republic*, 331.

is really indirect beneficence, but they seem rather to be ordinary conflicts of obligation.

§ 7. I am inclined, though with misgiving, to class closely with the obligation of promise-keeping that of veracity. Certainly they are not identical, for promising is not the mere expression of an intention. To volunteer or exchange information or to answer without protest a question which the questioner is entitled to put seems to imply a tacit understanding that truth will be told. This is in accordance with the common view that perjury, where the promise of veracity has been explicit, is only a worse form of lying.

The statement 'I promise' (that is 'I hereby place myself under an obligation'), like the statement 'I am making a statement', is one of those that can never be false; if it were false the man would have made no promise and therefore could not break one. The maker of the promise may intend to break it and may even think that he is unable to keep it, but he has nevertheless promised. A serious difficulty here is that if our description of a promise as 'putting oneself under an obligation' is correct, the man who promises the impossible puts himself under an obligation which he cannot fulfil. If he were in fact unable, but thought himself able, to keep the promise, he has put himself under the subjective obligation to try, and, when he has tried his best, his failure puts him under another obligation to provide the nearest substitute in his power. If at the times of both promising and paying he is convinced of the impossibility, he has put himself under obligations not only to provide the nearest substitute but also to recompense the creditor for the fraud. Perhaps his fault may best be described as a lie about the nature of the obligation under which he put himself; he said he was putting himself under an obligation which he does not believe he can be under; he really thereby puts himself under a different one. This sounds artificial but is, I believe, really true to our thought. If I discovered that a debtor had known when he incurred the debt that he had no assets, I should not say 'You ought to pay the money all the same', but some such thing as 'Well, you ought to give me a free day's work, or goods of more than the value, or pay me more later'. If both parties at the time of the promise believe the thing promised to be beyond control of the promiser, the transaction is farcical. 'I promise to love you till death' must be interpreted as 'I promise to try', and since success in any effort is seldom or never certain, some such condition is implicit in every promise, though here again failure may give rise to a new obligation. The most serious objection to defining a promise as putting oneself under an obligation is that in that case there would be no contradiction (as there seems to be at first sight) in saying 'I promise to pay but do not intend to do so'. It seems that a promise must be analysed into the putting of oneself under an obligation which one asserts or implies that one intends to fulfil. If it is simply the putting oneself under an obligation, the strict contradiction would be: 'I promise but recognize no obligation to keep promises'. Suppose I promise a man who I have no doubt is dying that when he is convalescent I will take him a sea-voyage. Should the unexpected happen, I am of course bound. I think that what I did was to imply a lie (as to my expectations, though not necessarily my intentions) by using the word 'when' instead of the word 'if', and perhaps by my confident tone of voice; if this lie caused him great happiness, even though it could not affect his recovery, I should think it my duty to tell it.

§ 8. Our reflective conscience agrees with the law more often than we suppose; it does so in recognizing the difference between a 'mere promise' and a bargain where some kind of 'consideration' is agreed if not received. The strongest such obligation is where a man has already done a useful bit of work for me or lent me something on promise of payment; if he has not yet started the job or handed over the cash, it is more venial to call it off; if he has already altered his plans or incurred other obligations in 'consideration' of the bargain, the obligation is strengthened though I have received no benefit. A promise, say, given to a puritanical parent never to travel on Sunday would be the weakest form; perhaps its obligation would be little more than that of veracity. A private 'pledge', such as a vow of abstinence or celibacy, can be no more than the expression of a resolution which if right[1] ought to be kept, and if wrong[1] or mistaken ought to be abandoned. A vow has been sometimes represented as a promise to God, but with God, I suppose, it is impossible to bargain. His will would always be that I ought[1] to do what was right in the circumstances whether I had vowed to do it or not to do it. A rather curious case is that of a promise to give a sum to a charity if others give like sums; here there is a consideration, but not one received by the promiser. It resembles the cases of 'consideration' such as inconvenience incurred by the other party but not benefiting me.

iii. *Restitution*

§ 9. Under retributive justice would come an obligation to apportion our benefits or improvements in favour of those who have benefited or improved *ourselves*, or, as the phrase goes, deserved well *of us*. I think the return of benefits and the return of improvements can be discussed on the same lines. The only question would be whether a benefit could be repaid by an improvement and vice versa, or each must be repaid in kind. Socrates thought education could not be paid. It has been questioned[2] if this alleged obligation is more than a natural inclination, comparable to that of

---

[1] As elsewhere, the argument is not affected by the insertion of 'objectively', 'subjectively', or 'putatively' before 'right' and 'wrong', if the same word is inserted before 'ought'.

[2] Godwin, *Political Justice*, consistently with his thorough-going utilitarianism.

vengeance as opposed to justice, though an amiable óne and perhaps virtuous. If it be an obligation it is one commonly overridden by one to apportion our benefits rather to needs and to desert. Sometimes, no doubt, the acceptance of a benefit may imply a tacit *promise* to return it, but I find it hard to say whether the adage that one good turn *deserves* another is more true or less when the first turn was done as a speculation. In the discussion of punishment[1] I said that, while punishment should always be inflicted, when possible, by an impartial agent, it seems particularly appropriate that reward should be conferred by the party benefited. The truth seems to be that we feel a special obligation to benefit not so much those who have benefited us as those who, we have reason to think, love us. If people have benefited us without expectation of reward that is a sign of love; and if they loved us they would have benefited us if they could, in which case we owe them as much as though they had more power to do so. This obligation could be defended even on the utilitarian ground that by an equal expenditure of money or energy we can give more pleasure to those who love us than to others, since it is a sign of returned affection. A present of no intrinsic worth is valued for the sake of the giver.

There is a much clearer obligation of this kind to recompense those we have injured, whether intentionally or by negligence. The special obligation, as distinct from inclination, we recognize, to our children, and in a less degree to our grandchildren, for whose existence we are partly responsible, seems to rest on the belief that life is a doubtful benefit; at any rate we have put them in an awkward situation which we ought to help them to deal with. We do not recognize any particular obligation to a man whose life we have saved, but rather one from him to us. The converse view, that children are indebted to their progenitors not only for

[1] Ch. V.

nurture but, nowadays at least, for the gratuity of birth, is more optimistic. Some theologians indeed have argued against birth control that it 'depopulates heaven'; whether they believe in eternal punishment and have calculated the chances and balanced the probable felicity and damage, I do not know. At any rate the same argument might be urged against celibacy.

B. IMPROVEMENT

§ 10. It has seldom been questioned that we have obligations to improve ourselves and others, to provide for all men good experiences and the opportunity of good activities. The question of the distribution of improvement has been discussed in this chapter under the headings of retributive and distributive justice. An enumeration of some good dispositions or virtues, which are capacities for good experiences and activities, was attempted in Chapter VII. It is by the cultivation of these capacities and the provision of the external conditions for their exercise that we can chiefly improve others as well as ourselves. For it is difficult to see how we can increase in others that eminent form of goodness moral desert. We may remove their temptations and make them more *inclined* to do their putative duties, as well as more apt to judge wisely what their subjective duties are, but this does not increase their moral desert. In theological language, the shortcomings of a man due to ignorance, bad environment, lack of moral precept and example, will not be accounted to him for unrighteousness by God. The puzzling question in what sense we can have or fulfil an obligation to make ourselves *morally* better must be postponed.[1]

C. BENEFICENCE

§ 11. I do not know that anyone who acknowledged any obligations has denied the disobligation to cause 'wanton'

---

[1] See Ch. XI, § 10.

pain, or the general obligation to relieve undeserved and useless pain, or the obligation to afford innocent pleasures. They have generally grounded these obligations upon the alleged goodness of happiness and the corresponding badness of its opposite, but since we have seen the difficulty of maintaining this view in any clear form,[1] I have preferred to distinguish separate obligations of beneficence and improvement. As we saw, in discussing this point, if happiness is to be promoted because of its goodness there would be as much obligation to produce it in ourselves, when equally deserved and equally useful, as in others. With this conclusion I am inclined to agree, though I am not confident of the premiss that happiness can be called unconditionally good; but I reserve this point for the next chapter.

The undisputed fact that our obligation to produce happiness is regulated by those of distributive and retributive justice might suggest that it is not grounded on an unconditional goodness of happiness, which would, if that were so, be equally good whoever had it. But our obligations with regard to other things confessedly good, such as virtuous dispositions, might also be subject to such regulation,[2] and this might suggest that these obligations, too, are grounded not on the goodness of the states or activities promoted, but on the fact that they are also generally desirable or a source of happiness, so that the obligations would not be of improvement but of beneficence. I do not think this is convincing. It might be that both happiness and virtuous activities are good and that we have a consequent obligation to increase their total amount, but that, since they are also desirable, we have a possibly conflicting obligation to distribute them equally or in proportion to merit. The question whether men necessarily desire instances of goodness to occur in themselves will be discussed in a later chapter.[3]

[1] See Ch. VIII.   [2] But see § 5, above.   [3] Ch. XI, §§ 6, 7.

D. OTHER OBLIGATIONS

§ 12. There is another obligation which I recognize, that of non-interference, corresponding to the claim of liberty; but I am uncertain whether to class it as a branch of beneficence or as distinct. We were inclined to say[1] that men have a 'natural claim' to an equal share of liberty, that is to the power of doing what they would choose, unhampered by our physical coercion or intimidation. Such freedom is no doubt a considerable ingredient of happiness, but we may often believe that a man would be happier if some of his strong impulses were curbed; we then find a conflict between the obligations of beneficence and of non-interference.

It may have been this consideration which recommended to the utilitarians the term 'greatest happiness' rather than 'pleasure' or 'satisfaction' simply, for a particular pleasure may be detrimental to happiness, though the greatest possible sum of pleasures or satisfactions would be identical with the greatest happiness. If so, their contention was that I have a disobligation to satisfy a man's impulse or mistaken policy which will not make for his happiness on the whole. Yet against this is the strong conviction that sane adults have a claim to freedom, so that we have a corresponding obligation to non-interference, and even to prevent interference by others; an obligation not to be identified with any of those enumerated—beneficence, improvement, or justice. Perhaps the solution is that, in general, every sane adult is the best judge of his own happiness, and that such pains as he may incur by an impulsive or ignorant pursuit of it are usually less than those of a restraint which, however wise, he will regard as an oppressive frustration.

§ 13. It is often suggested that there is another obligation which seems different from those enumerated though presupposing them, and which I find hard to understand and

---

[1] See Chs. VI and XV.

consequently to classify. It is sometimes called the obligation of 'playing the game'. It is alleged that I sometimes have an obligation to do or forbear something (though my so behaving will have no good or felicific result and will fulfil no claim) provided that *if* all or many other persons acted in the same way, good results or the fulfilment of claims would ensue; and this obligation is not thought to depend on the possibility of my behaviour being an example.

Suppose that on election day I have important business which must be neglected if I go to the poll. The chances that my vote will affect the issue are perhaps one to ten thousand, and perhaps nobody can know whether I vote or not. Yet some would say: 'Still, you ought to vote, for, if all or most did not, democracy would collapse'. Or, to take a negative instance, it might be said: 'You should not make the short cut across the grass even alone and after dark, for if everybody did so the lawn would be spoilt.'[1]

Yet in cases that look closely parallel we do not think there is any obligation. If a man could only be ransomed from brigands for £1,000 and I could only find £100, I should feel no obligation to send this to the bandit chief unless the other £900 could be raised. Or, to take a negative instance, I do not feel any obligation to keep off Sgurr-nan-Gillean because if everybody went there the place would be spoilt. People who make it a condition of subscribing to a charity that other people *shall* subscribe enough to make the scheme a success clearly do not believe in playing the game. This difficulty bears some relation to the puzzle about cumulative effects: 'excessive smoking is harmful but

[1] Kant in the *Fundamental Principles of the Metaphysic of Morals* says that the categorical imperative or formula of duty is 'Never so act that you cannot without contradiction at the same time will that all men should act on the same maxim'. He applies this plausibly to lying, since if everybody lied deception would at least be difficult. But his other examples (suicide, idleness, unkindness) do not exemplify his formula and suggest that he really had in mind the situations I am describing.

one more cigarette can do you no harm'. I do not know whether there really is such an obligation, and therefore cannot classify it; I do not see how an actual obligation can depend upon any unfulfilled condition (whose fulfilment may be very improbable), but only on a condition which my action itself will fulfil, as when I say, 'If I do this (as I can) it will set a good example'.[1] Objectively the capacity to produce something good gives rise to an obligation to produce it, and subjectively the belief in such capacity gives rise to an obligation to try. This was probably what was meant by saying that 'the good is what ought to exist', but it is hard to see how any state or quality can 'owe' or have duties, especially a quality of something which does not exist.

§ 14. In this sketch of a classification in which our obligations might be arranged, I have not thought it necessary always to repeat that an instance of any one class might conflict either with another instance of the same (one promise with another) or with an instance of a different class (a promise with a possibility of beneficence).

Moreover, it has to be borne in mind that all moral decisions are in the nature of a gamble or, to speak less profanely, of an insurance. This results from the fact that we can never know the situation in which we are or the results of what we do; at best we can only know our subjective obligations; our putative duty is to do what we think demanded by what seem most likely to be the facts and the consequences. If during an air-raid I meet a car running towards a crater, though I may assume it is on urgent business, yet, if I feel sure there are no turnings between it and the pitfall, I confidently judge I ought to stop it; if I know there are a hundred cross-roads intervening, certainly not; if four or ten, nobody can say.

§ 15. Even with all these qualifications, the classification will be justly criticized at once for its overlapping or

---

[1] Or 'I am capable of setting a good example'.

indistinct boundaries and for its exaggerated contrasts. It is unsatisfactory as theory and fortunately superfluous for practice. Nothing of it need be explicitly present to our minds when we decide a question of casuistry,[1] any more than are the laws of optics and perspective when we judge the size and shape of distant bodies.

I said before that we must not assume all our obligations to be deducible from one ultimate ground, though it is proper to consider the possibility; and the same is true of the question whether they can be reduced to two or three species, or must be left as individual members of a genus which is also an *ultima species*. The inadequacy of my own attempt at such reduction is surely no proof of its impossibility; but the like weakness of all other attempts which I have met with begins to make the impossibility probable. We might have done better to remember Bishop Butler's ironical stricture[2] on such codifications of the moral law as a fit occupation for 'persons of leisure' in 'many respects of great service'.

'Yet', he goes on, 'let any plain honest man before he engages in any course of action, ask himself, Is this I am going about right or is it wrong? . . . I do not in the least doubt but that this question would be answered agreeably to truth and virtue by almost any fair man in almost any circumstance. Neither do there appear any cases which look like exceptions to this; but those of superstition and of partiality to ourselves. Superstition may, perhaps,. be somewhat of an exception; but partiality to ourselves is not, this being itself dishonesty.'

This is an exaggeration, as we have seen,[3] even though he is only speaking of subjective duties or, as he says, though 'the intended consequences alone are to be considered, since they make the action what it is'. That no party to a quarrel is ever honestly mistaken through partiality to himself, or more often to his country, his party, his class, his friends, his sect, is a rash claim which Butler modifies by

---

[1] See Ch. I, § 5.   [2] *Sermons*, iii.   [3] Ch. II.

the warning against accepting popular prejudices without question, though perhaps this comes rather under the head of superstition.

§ 16. That we often mistake for obligations mere 'superstitions' associated with religion, with class distinctions, with sex taboos, and with national prejudices, or merely with our nurse's taste in manners has already been noticed.[1] It is perhaps as a help in dispelling such superstitions that the kind of classification I have been attempting has some value. The reflection which either confirms or refutes something that we had taken for granted is aided by the questions: What is the ground of this alleged obligation? Has it one shared with others or is it unique?

My headings of obligation were: (1) Justice Distributive and Retributive (Rewards and Punishment, Debts, Veracity, Benefits); (2) Improvement; and (3) Beneficence (under which I doubtfully included non-interference); about 'playing the game' I reached no decision. I reserve for the next chapter the question whether beneficence is purely altruistic or there is an obligation to seek happiness also for ourselves.

[1] Ch. III, § 4.

X

PRUDENCE

§ 1. It is generally admitted that we have obligations to improve both ourselves and others and also to benefit others; in the eighteenth century it was assumed[1] that we had at least as strong an obligation to provide for our own happiness as for that of other men, and this view was retained by the utilitarians, but to-day it is seriously questioned.[2] On the utilitarian theory, that our duty to produce the maximum amount of happiness was founded on the goodness of happiness, the older view was inevitable, since what is good in one man is *ceteris paribus* as good in another. This view cannot be ruled out by a general assertion that we have no direct duties to ourselves, for the generally admitted obligation to cultivate and exercise our capacities for good activities cannot always be founded on any probable advantage to others, and none need ensue. A man who foresees lifelong solitude, say on a desert island, has certainly far fewer obligations than one in society, but it is paradoxical to say he has none.

A curious result, not always noticed by those who combined the doctrines of heavenly reward and of the obligation to self-beneficence, would be that anybody who performs any putative duty from the conscientious motive is thereby, perhaps unconsciously, fulfilling an objective obligation to further his happiness upon the whole; he would be acquiring merit for which there was a certain reward.

§ 2. If the belief in an obligation to pursue one's own

---

[1] Even by strict moralists like Butler (*Sermons*) and Price (*Review*).

[2] Probably the change was due to Kant, who holds that we have no such obligation except so far as happiness may make us more useful to our neighbours, and, as he rather suspiciously adds, so far as it may save us from temptations. It does save us from some but leads us into others. The prevalence of the older view in a theistic period may have been due to the desire to make it our duty to deserve heaven.

happiness on the whole rather than to yield to pressing impulses be an illusion, I know of no illusion in the moral sphere which, to judge from ordinary language, is so common. 'He *deserves* what has happened to him; he knew he was acting imprudently'; 'He *deserves* neither pity nor help, he brought it on himself with his eyes open'; 'I have a duty to myself' (in the way of prudence).

If we have such an obligation it is one that is very commonly overridden by stronger obligations to our neighbours and one that needs little emphasis, being commonly exaggerated because it always coincides with a strong desire, though not always with the strongest.

Do we, then, feel remorse for a past act of conscious imprudence or only regret, like that for ignorance or maladroitness? I incline, after hesitation, to say that we feel remorse; that we speak accurately when we say 'I have only myself to blame'. We think we ought not to sacrifice the happiness of our lifetime[1] to some trivial satisfaction of others. What is it that here overrides our obligation to altruistic beneficence? I certainly do not think I ought to keep some casual promise, such as to play tennis, at the cost of the treat of my life; I am inclined to say I ought *not*; I should certainly call it 'unreasonable'. What here overrides the obligation of promise keeping? It will not do to say that I have a claim but no obligation in such cases, for a claim without a correlative obligation could not override an obligation, and if there is an obligation to act prudently it must be an obligation of myself to myself. This is no doubt a kind of obligation which arouses criticism, but like the less questionable obligation of self-improvement it might seem to be an obligation of myself at one time to myself at another.

I admit that it is also paradoxical to say that we should always have a *duty*, where no obligation of justice intervened, to sacrifice a less satisfaction of others to a greater of our own.

[1] A sympathetic instance is Anne Elliot in Jane Austen's *Persuasion*.

And it may be said: 'Surely I can do what I choose with my own: if I have a right to it, I may give it away when I choose.' And we do sometimes praise a man for sacrificing his own enjoyments to the *slightly* lesser ones of other people. Yet, on the other hand, why should we praise him for doing what he has a perfect right not to do and therefore no obligation to do?

§ 3. We are involved here in the puzzle about 'works of supererogation' or the 'laxer duties' of generosity as opposed to the 'stricter' ones of justice. Such phrases imply that there are morally praiseworthy acts which I am not, in strictness, morally obliged to do, presumably because I have a right not to. I admittedly deserve esteem for paying my debts when I might safely default: 'An *honest* man is the noblest work of God.' Yet perhaps I might deserve no less if I gave to others not only what I owed, nor even gratuitously of my abundance, but what I needed as much or more than they did. To the questions 'Am I my brother's keeper?' and 'Must I bear his burdens?' the answers sometimes seem to be 'Yes'.

We have admitted that the duties of justice differ from those of beneficence and improvement in having a different ground, but we cannot say that we must always be just before we are generous, since we may have a stronger obligation to relieve a starving stranger than to pay a debt.[1] Can we find any place for these alleged 'works of supererogation' which go beyond our duties of beneficence by decreasing our own happiness more than they increase anybody else's? In what can the goodness of an act consist which is not done because it is thought a duty, and which it is thought may produce less satisfaction in the recipient than is sacrificed by the donor? Have the recipients any claim to such free gifts? Has not the donor a stronger claim to choose his own greater satisfaction

[1] Contrast Kant on 'strict' and 'lax' obligations, *Fundamental Principles of the Metaphysic of Morals*, ii.

before their less? If he has, it would seem wrong not to satisfy this stronger claim. The best answer I can give is that if a man actually takes more pleasure in giving away his ration to a less hungry man than in eating it, this must result from a very good, because sympathetic, disposition; but in such a case the question does not arise; the man is not sacrificing a greater satisfaction, he is taking one.

§ 4. I suggest then, though without great confidence, that there is never a direct duty to increase the satisfaction of others at the cost of a greater or equal loss to oneself, but that we might have an indirect obligation or even duty to do such actions because likely to improve our character by cultivating sympathy; and in the absence of a stronger incompatible obligation, this might be a duty. 'Works of supererogation', then, would be obligations of self-improvement, not of beneficence or of other improvement; if anybody has a correlative claim that they should be done, it must be the agent himself.

XI

RELATION OF GOODNESS AND
OBLIGATION TO DESIRE AND CHOICE

§ 1. I HAVE said[1] that ethical goodness, as distinct from utility or advantageousness, is a quality of some conscious states or activities, and it may be called an intrinsic[2] quality as opposed to a 'relational' one, to distinguish it from so-called qualities like pleasantness, nearness, utility, familiarity, connexion, which are really relations to something else whether that something else is conscious or not. The good-ness of anything, then, does not result from any desire for its possession or existence nor from any satisfaction caused by its possession or existence. It need not be added that a thing's goodness cannot depend upon its being thought or known to be good; no quality could thus depend, for nothing can be known to exist which does not exist already, and the belief that anything exists may be false. We may know or believe that if something should exist it will be good provided we know or believe that such things always have characters which make them good. The idea that there is nothing good or bad, but thinking makes it so, has seemed plausible be-cause only conscious states can be good, so that what is good is always something of whose existence some creature is aware; but other creatures who become aware of this state might not desire its continuance, and even the creature in whom it occurs may not reflect that it is good, and, if he does, may much more strongly desire something incompatible with it. Hard thinking, for instance, may be good; I cannot think hard without being aware of it, but nobody else need be; I need not have decided that it is good or may even have

[1] Ch. VI, § 4.
[2] Or 'absolute'. Cf. Moore, *Principia Ethica*, § 6, &c., and Ross, *The Right and the Good*, iv.

taken for granted that it is not; those who want to outwit me may wish me to stop and I myself may desire rather to doze.

i. *Existence of Goods*

§ 2. Must the belief that something is or would be good always arouse some degree of desire that it should exist? I do not see the same necessity for this connexion as I do between thinking something would be good and thinking that I am under an obligation, if possible, to produce it.[1] I can only offer an empirical report of introspection, which is notoriously fallible, and of other people's self-revelation whose minds I cannot examine. I seem to find that when I think something other than conscientious action good I always have some desire that it should exist, though I may much more strongly desire something incompatible. I prefer that anybody should be generous unless it prevents him being useful to me; that he should be clear-minded unless it exposes my dullness or prevents me overreaching him; that he should have good taste unless it makes him outbid me at an auction.

§ 3. But the relation of the eminently good thing called conscientious action to my desires is less clear. I no doubt prefer a judge to decide conscientiously unless it involves my damage or what I regard as a very grievous injustice, in either of which cases I might try to bribe him. But when the conscientious act would cause the agent much pain (which seems to increase its goodness) and would fail in its purpose (which makes it no worse), as when a man might be burned in trying to rescue the inhabitants of a burning house that was in fact empty, I do not desire such a complex to be realized. Is this merely an instance of a weak desire that conscientious actions should occur being swamped by a stronger one that pain should not? And if so, does it imply that the pain is evil and here bad enough to outweigh the

---

[1] Or 'that my capacity to produce something good obliges me to do so'.

moral good, or only that I am more sympathetic than philagathist?

I might sometimes desire that, once the situation has arisen in which a man falsely thinks he ought to be a martyr, a martyrdom should be endured, because this is good, but I might more strongly desire that the pain should not occur and that therefore the situation making that good possible should not arise.

§ 4. No doubt our attitudes to past pains, of others as well as of ourselves, differ from those to future ones more than our attitudes to past and future goods differ, though there is a strange prejudice that progress in goodness is better than degeneration even when the total good is no greater.[1] I am not sure whether I wish a tale of old, unhappy heroism were true. Perhaps this conflict between sympathy with pain and appreciation of goodness accounts for our mixed 'enjoyment' of tragedy and shrinking from it, as if we ought to desire it more than we do.

Even apart from sympathetic feelings, the desire that because of its goodness a painful heroic act should be done would conflict with a desire that another alleged good should occur, namely the proportioning of happiness to merit. So we get the paradox that the very painfulness which contributes to the goodness of the conscientious act, and so far should make its occurrence desirable, also contributes to the badness of the complex whole (a good man in pain) and so far makes it undesirable. I think I might be slightly less anxious to escape a pain inflicted upon me because, as I agreed, it was deserved than one inflicted arbitrarily.

---

[1] Probably because we believe that the past has been pretty bad. But I cannot see that the goodness of a man's later life is any better than that of his youth, and the same applies to the history of our race. Cf. Lotze, *Mikrokosmus*, vii. But contrast D'Houteville, *Essai sur la Providence*, 'C'est l'avenir surtout qui a été le grand objet de Dieu dans la création, et c'est pour cet avenir seul que le présent existe.' But every future will one day be present.

But, as already hinted, my desire that something good should exist may be overridden in other ways. If, owing to miscalculation, the heroic act should result in no pain to the agent but much to others, I should wish the whole complex not to occur even though I and my friends were not among the sufferers. It looks as if the best complex of this kind would be a conscientious act done in the mistaken belief that it would cause the agent a great overbalance of pain, but which in fact caused him (as well as the deserving persons he intended to benefit) a great over-balance of happiness; for instance, the act of a martyr to a good cause who falsely believed that he would get no reward in this life or another; the only element of the badness in the whole would be that of a false and unpleasant belief.

I conclude that I always have some desire that good things other than conscientious actions should exist, though I may have a stronger desire for something incompatible; that I always have some desire that a conscientious action should be done on an occasion which demands it, though I may have a stronger desire that the pain inseparable from the action, whether to the agent, to myself, or to others should not occur; that I do not desire the occurrence of a situation in which very painful action would become a duty either for myself or others, though I do find some satisfaction in past conscientious actions, whether my own or not, which were very painful to the agent and perhaps to others.

ii. *Contemplation of Goods*

§ 5. A second question about the relation of goodness to desire and satisfaction is here plainly indicated. Do we desire to contemplate good things? Though I may desire that good things should exist, I shall get the satisfaction of this desire not by their existence but only by knowledge or belief of it, and only at the time when such knowledge or belief is actualized, that is to say when I am contemplating them.

I certainly desire the welfare of my children and of the world
after my death; I only get any satisfaction so far as I can
believe that welfare probable; I should get more if I could
know it certain; most, I suppose, if faith should vanish into
sight.

If I think the appreciation of 'good' music good and consequently desire it to occur and subscribe to free concerts,
I surely want to watch other people's enjoyment and hear
their applause. It has been suggested that this desire for the
contemplation of what is good is itself an instance of desire
that what is good should exist, since the contemplation of
what is good is itself good. But this seems a mistake for
several reasons: I generally desire to contemplate the existence of anything, good or not, which I desire to exist, such
as the humiliation of my enemy; I desire to contemplate a
good in the near future or present much more than in the
remote future or past, though the date of an occurrence cannot vary its goodness; if the contemplation were desired to
occur because of its goodness it would be desired for others
as much as for myself; lastly, it is not the contemplation
of good but only its pleased contemplation[1] that could be
itself good as would also be the displeased contemplation of
evil, which nobody desires to have.[2] So I must first think I
shall take pleasure in the contemplation and must desire it
before I can think it good. We have remarked that the pleased
contemplation of other people's pleasure and the pained contemplation of their pain, even of deserved pain, is good, but
I should more desire the absence of the pain or even, if it is
incurable, to be ignorant of it. It is relevant to add here that
if pleasure is good the pleased contemplation of my own

---

[1] Ross, *Foundations of Ethics*, p. 283.

[2] If there must be incurable evil it would be good that nobody should
contemplate it; but since nothing is evil except conscious states or
activities, their owners must be aware of them. If they do not think them
evil such ignorance is bad; if they do, it is better their contemplation
should be painful, and we desire it should be.

pleasure would be good; and I think we do find some goodness in the capacity, even among the discontents of age, to
prize rather than regret memories of a happy youth.

iii. *Possession of Goods*

§ 6. If it be allowed that we always have some desire for
the existence of what is good and for its contemplation, we
come to the last and most vital question about the relation
of good to desire. Do we specially desire that activities or
states which we think good should occur in our own lives?[1]
This is a question which has caused as much fundamental
controversy in ethics as any other. I may certainly think the
appreciation of good music good *and also* desire to hear a
concert myself more than that another should, even if I
thought he would appreciate it more; but this evidently
could not be a desire aroused by the thought that the appreciation is good, since his is thought better. The appreciation
of good music is pleasant, for hearing it without pleasure
would not be appreciation, and that must be why I desire it

---

[1] Aristotle, *Nicomachean Ethics*, 1170^{b}2, 'It is pleasant to see what is
good in oneself'; and 1169^{a}17, πᾶς γὰρ νοῦς αἱρεῖται τὸ βέλτιστον ἑαυτῷ.
The last passage is characteristically ambiguous; it may mean 'Every
intelligent being chooses for itself what is best', or 'chooses what is best
for it', i.e. most advantageous. The question is posed with like ambiguity
by Plato (*Symposium* 204*e*, 206*a*): 'Men desire nothing except the good.
. . . But then, he replied, can we so simply say that men desire the good?
Yes, I replied. What? said he, must we not add that they also desire the
good for themselves? (εἶναι τὸ ἀγαθὸν αὐτοῖς). . . . All men always desire
that good things should be theirs.' Kant (*Critique of Practical Reason*,
trans. Abbot, ii) distinguishes *das Gute*, which reason tells us we ought
to desire because it is good, from *das Wohl*, which may be called weal or
well-being because we desire it or it satisfies us. He points out that in the
formula *Nihil appetimus nisi sub ratione boni*, 'We desire nothing except
as good', not only is *boni* ambiguous (as between *das Gute* and *das Wohl*)
but also *sub ratione*. The sentence might mean 'Whatever we desire we
then conceive/to be good' or 'We never desire anything unless we have
first conceived it to be good'. Neither is plausible if *bonum* means *das
Gute* and only the first if it means *das Wohl*. It is not here clear how Kant
would answer the question in the text above. Cf. Ch. VII, § 1.

rather for myself. This was probably what hedonistic utilitarians had in mind when they argued, in unfortunate phrase, that since pleasure is good, it is 'irrational' to desire it more for oneself than for others.[1] They meant that it is self-contradictory to say that I desire something to occur simply because of its goodness, yet more desire it to occur where it would be no better but perhaps less good. The desire to hear music is not 'instinctive' like hunger but 'reflective', dependent upon memory of past pleasantness, and desires conditioned in some such way seem to be common to 'irrational' creatures, while the desire that what is good should exist does not.

§ 7. There now, however, recurs for consideration the more difficult case of good activities which, instead of being also pleasant, can be painful to the agent; and we may as well at once take the eminently good activity of conscientious action, and ask whether we always desire to do such actions especially ourselves because of their goodness.

We have seen that the utilitarians held that our one duty is to produce good,[2] and some of them, paradoxically identifying this doctrine with egoistic hedonism, claimed that this is always to the agent's 'good' or advantage,[3] and even went on, identifying it also with psychological hedonism, to assert that the motive of every action is a desire for this 'good' of the agent, a good misconceived in 'bad' actions, correctly calculated in 'good' ones.[4] But as I have repeated rather wearisomely what is good in me would be equally good in you,

[1] Sidgwick (*Methods of Ethics*) sometimes inconsistently denies this. Cf. Moore, *Principia Ethica*, § 59.

[2] Ch. IV, § 10.

[3] Ibid. Cf. Joseph, *Problems of Ethics*, especially pp. 133–4. Cf. my British Academy Lecture (Hertz, 1937), *An Ambiguity in the Word Good*.

[4] T. H. Green, *Prolegomena to Ethics*, §§ 91–2: 'The motive in every imputable act . . . is a desire for personal good. . . . It is superfluous to add good *to himself*; for anything conceived as good in such a way that the agent acts for the sake of it must be conceived as *his own* good.'

but what is to your greatest advantage or satisfaction may not be to mine. I think the religious mystic does not envy the goodness of God, unattainable by himself, nor does he think that God is jealous of the meritorious resistance to temptation by his creatures, a goodness alien to divine nature. Few things are more grievous and depressing than a quarrel between those one loves. One is apt to comfort oneself with the reflection: 'I had no part in it, I cannot blame myself.' But further reflection suggests that this is a selfish thought. One or, more likely, both parties are to blame and now embittered. What could be worse?

So far, then, as a man desires the existence of what is good for the sake of its goodness, he desires the performance of conscientious actions no matter by whom. 'To be great-minded a man must not delight in himself or his own, but in justice whether done by himself or by another.'[1]

§ 8. Doubtless I am in fact specially attracted in some degree by the general thought of conscientious actions done by myself or those dear to me, just as I more desire to hear a concert myself than that a stranger should; and I take more satisfaction in having done such an action than in hearing that he has, as I might in a poem I had written myself or a picture I had bought; but this extra satisfaction would not be in any greater goodness. Such desires and satisfactions cannot arise from love of what is good, but rather from a form of pride or rivalry, the desire to possess oneself what is esteemed by others and arouses in them the mixed feelings of envy and sympathetic pleasure. Pride indeed, including both the 'search for a reputation and a name' and secret self-congratulation, was Hume's analysis of what he oddly calls 'our interested obligation to virtue'.[2] If we always followed 'interest' or desire we might sometimes be moved by the desire of reputation or of an easy conscience to do what con-

---

[1] Plato, *Laws*, 732*a*.
[2] Hume, *Enquiry*, IX. ii; *Treatise*, III. ii. 2.

science enjoined; but we often desire more than the approval of conscience something incompatible with it and think we can so carry it in public as to preserve our reputation and our name; yet the disinterested obligation remains and we can fulfil it.

§ 9. We have seen[1] that we sometimes think we ought to do actions because they are just and not because they will have good results; also[2] that the reason why we ought to do an action can never be the goodness of the action itself since it would have none if done from a bad motive, and *any* action would be good if done from a good one. How, then, have philosophers persuaded themselves that our only duty is to increase good and that our motive is always the desire for our own good or satisfaction?[3] They have thought, as I do, that we always have *some* desire that good actions should occur and *some* satisfaction in thinking they have occurred; and they have seen, what is indisputable, that I can only cause such actions, and only know of them, in myself. And they have falsely concluded that I shall always get *most* satisfaction by acting conscientiously. They have overlooked the fact that I commonly desire much more strongly than the occurrence of a conscientious action something incompatible with it, such as to avoid pain, and also the fact that my remorse for not doing my duty is different from my dissatisfaction in other people not doing theirs, though the two failures are equally bad.

§ 10. The remaining element of truth in their contention is puzzling: if I think I have a duty I must on reflection know that to do it for that reason would be good, and I must then have some desire that this good should occur. So it might seem that I can never do anything simply because it is my putative duty uninfluenced by this desire; and if this desire is my motive, being stronger than any desire for anything incompatible, then the action, though it may be virtuous and

[1] Ch. IV, § 18.   [2] Ibid., § 21.   [3] Ch. III, §§ 8, 9.

good, is not conscientious or moral, though I should not have desired to do it had I not first believed I ought. Something of this kind does sometimes seem to go on in my mind: I may hesitate to do a putative duty, especially one of beneficence or improvement, to which I have a strong disinclination; but I may then reflect that such acts are good, morally good if done because thought duties, virtuous if done from a desire that the good should exist. In this situation my original putative duty to do the act as just or optimific would be reinforced by a distinguishable though concurrent obligation to do it as optimizing. I might then choose[1] to fulfil this reinforced obligation without further reflection, though I still desired more to do something incompatible (when it would be a conscientious action); or I might choose to gratify my incompatible desire; or I might continue to reflect on the goodness of fulfilling the reinforced obligation, which would again reinforce it either until the cumulative goodness aroused a preponderant desire (and then I should behave virtuously) or until it was too late. I could not go on *ad infinitum* because it would certainly be too late when I died.

I should, however, maintain that we often choose to do actions (especially perhaps those of justice) simply because we believe them to be duties without reflecting that doing them for that reason would be good, or at least when the desire for the occurrence of such a good is much weaker than the desire to do something incompatible.

An action done simply because it is a putative duty has perhaps some goodness, even though there is no conflicting desire; it is done for a reason, namely that I have a more or less well-grounded belief that it is my duty, and not to do it would be to act contrary to this belief. An instance would be when, as examiner, I have considered the papers and, having no interest in the candidates, I give the best mark to the one I think best.

[1] See next chapter.

§ 11. This discussion is more important than at first sight it may seem. I believe this puzzling relation between the belief in a duty and the thought that to fulfil it for that reason would be good was in the minds of those who have held that what makes me think any act my duty is always the belief that it will be optimizing. In this they were clearly wrong. As we have seen, and as some of them admitted,[1] I may think an action a duty which I do not think optimific; and I could not think such an action optimizing unless I thought of it as done because I already believed it my duty; so I could not think it my duty because I thought it good. They were also clearly wrong when they went on to assert[2] that the production of goodness or even of my own goodness is always the production of 'my own good', for that term is generally used to mean my happiness or satisfaction or advantage. If I asked whether it would be more for my own good to invest my money or to buy an annuity, nobody would suppose I was asking which would be a conscientious act or which would manifest a virtuous disposition, that is to say which would be the better act. What led moralists into this misuse of language was probably the fact that I can only produce that eminently good thing, a painful conscientious action, in myself; to produce a situation where such an act is possible for another is to lead him into temptation, and to put myself in the way of temptation is presumptuous. This is true; but we must reply that being done by myself makes no difference to the goodness of a conscientious action but may make much to my good. The capacity to produce good involves an obligation to do so, and there is one kind of good I can only produce in myself; those actions are *morally* best which are done, though they are thought preponderatingly undesirable, because they are thought duties, not those which

[1] e.g. Joseph, *Problems of Ethics*, cited above, Ch. III, § 9, and cf. Ch. IV, § 21.
[2] See Ch. III, §§ 8, 9.

are done from a preponderating desire that something good should exist.

This is the best account I can give of the relation of obligations and of goodness to desire. One question remains as to the relation of obligation and desire to choice. Must I always 'choose' to do what I happen at the moment most to desire, whether that be to do my duty or something inconsistent with it, or is my choice, at least between doing my duty and what I more desire, undetermined, spontaneous, free?

XII

FREEDOM

§ 1. No question has been more or more deservedly debated in morals than that of the freedom of the will. On the one side stand both the axiom that every event must have a cause and the empirical facts that we often, with some confidence, predict the behaviour of individuals even from our superficial knowledge of their character, and of groups from an actuarial calculation of averages. On the other side are the two corresponding arguments that since 'ought implies can' there could be no morality without freedom, and that we have a direct introspective certainty of freedom whenever we act.

We are not here in the least concerned with political or social freedom;[1] that is to say freedom from physical coercion or intimidation by other men, but solely with moral freedom of choice in any situation whether of much or little social freedom. Nor are we concerned with so-called 'freedom from passion'. A moral being without passions would necessarily behave morally, as a creature with passions but no conscience necessarily follows its strongest desire, and no question of freedom would arise for either. In any conflict between conscience and passion if those who obey conscience are free, so are those who obey passion; both are responsible for a free choice. The whole question has been confused by a Hegelian[2] doctrine invented, I cannot help thinking, in the interest of a political theory, that moral freedom of choice would be 'mere caprice', and that the only true freedom of which man is capable consists in obedience (preferably willing) to the laws (preferably good) of a state.

---

[1] See Ch. XV. ii.
[2] *Philosophie des Rechts* (trans. Knox), §§ 15 note, 140 e, 206, and *Phenomenologie des Geistes* (trans. Baillie), C(AA)B. Cf. below, Ch. XV. ii, § 7 note.

Clearly those who defend freedom need have no intention of denying causality except for actions; indeed it is by freedom that they would distinguish an action from an event. The circulation of my blood, a sneeze, a fit of anger, the involuntary recollection of a tune are events. The determinist, I suppose, would distinguish actions as the foreseen mental or bodily changes caused by desire, as when I pick a blackberry, attend to the striking of a clock, or risk my life for a friend's; and he would add, with truth, that all desires and all beliefs, which may condition them, are caused by our inborn capacities, past history, and present situation. The agent's belief in a duty is caused by the apparent situation and his capacity for moral thinking; his desire, which may be contrary to it, is caused in other ways; but neither of these when they conflict necessitates his choice. He chooses freely. The result is either a moral act or an immoral one with some consequent remorse. It is just because we presume that animals always follow their strongest desire that we agree they cannot be free.

§ 2. It has been suggested that the case for freedom is in fact strengthened by contemporary physical theories of the unpredictable behaviour of individual electrons. Of this the layman can only say that it is hard to see why the fact that we cannot discover the causes of individual changes, whose occurrence we have inferred by relying on the law of causality, should entitle us to assert that they are uncaused.[1] It would be absurd to argue that merely because we do not know enough to predict certainly our own or other people's behaviour, or the splashes of a waterfall, or to-morrow's weather, these must be uncaused. If the electronic changes were in fact uncaused, they would have to be ascribed either to a wholly mythical 'chance' or to the free will of rational beings like ourselves not subject to constraining forces or

[1] 'Incompletely determined' is the usual phrase. But what was incompletely determined would contain an uncaused element. Cf. § 10, below.

desires. Electrons would be moral beings. The older analogy from organic behaviour, though inconclusive for freedom, was less inapt than this from physics.

§ 3. There is no reason to maintain that all our so-called 'choices' are free. If two dishes are set before me, equally wholesome, of which I can only take one, I surely must take the one I want more unless some ground of choice other than desire is introduced. I could not 'choose' the one I less wanted for that reason or for no reason. If I were dared to eat the one I loathed, I might, as a schoolboy, want to show my toughness more than to enjoy a delicacy, but I should still be doing what I most desired unless I thought that one ought to be tough. In taking the one I most desire to take I shall no doubt 'feel free' in the sense that I am doing just what I most want without coercion or intimidation, and this is sometimes called 'self-determination', but it is not freedom to choose either of alternatives. Since my desires and beliefs are all determined, my act could be predicted by anyone who could completely know my situation, my character, and my history.

But if I hear that there is not enough of the dish I prefer for two and that some invalid also prefers it, I might think I ought to leave it for him, and then indeed arises the question whether I can freely choose. If we ever think it our duty to provide for our own happiness on the whole rather than to satisfy a more urgent incompatible desire,[1] such a collision would of course be an instance of free choice, but not if it is merely a collision of desires.

The determinist will answer that, if I desire to do what I think my duty more than to savour the dish, I must do so, but as soon as the latter desire, growing with appetite, becomes stronger, I must obey it, and conversely, if a desire weakens with age or satiety and my moral convictions remain unchanged, I become more meritorious. He will contend that

[1] Ch. X.

this does not affect the fact that we have duties or believe we have, but since, on his view, we never could have chosen otherwise than we did, praise, blame, remorse, in the usual sense of these words, are sentiments which rest upon an illusion. We might indeed dislike a man for dishonesty or brutality, as we might for being a bore, and perhaps our dislike would be stronger; we might be ashamed of the same traits in ourselves, as we are of not seeing a joke or not enjoying Dante, and might try to conceal our dullness; but all this is not blame or remorse. The determinists would say that just as I may recognize a fine vintage but want beer more and therefore have to take beer, so I may think I have an obligation but am unable to fulfil it if I have a stronger conflicting desire. I have admitted that a desire to do one's duty as such occurs, probably much more often and more strongly in some men than others; and when this is stronger than any incompatible desire, or when there is a predominant desire from other causes to do what in fact we think our duty, there is no reason to call the choice free. But I would insist that it is possible to act when one more desires to refrain, simply from 'reverence' or 'respect' for the 'moral law',[1] which is merely an awkward phrase for thinking it one's duty. The thought that one is under an obligation to do something even sometimes in some degree disinclines one to do it. I have sometimes found it irksome to read or write on subjects which interest me when I was endowed as a scholar or lecturer to study them; and it has been rather scandalously suggested that

> Love, free love, can not be bound
> To any tree that grows on ground.[2]

§ 4. If we really believed that, our nature and history being what they are, there is only one act we can do on a given

---

[1] Kant, *Foundations of the Metaphysic of Morals*. He also calls this the only spontaneous (*selbst-bewirktes*) ground of action.
[2] Blake, *In a Myrtle Shade*.

occasion, should we not cease to think anything our duty, or rather would not the word lose its meaning? It is generally allowed that some kinds of incapacity preclude all obligation, as that it cannot be my duty to lift a ton; and this preclusion is not confined to physical impossibilities, since it cannot be my duty to solve immediately a complicated mathematical problem. Some, and among them determinists, have argued,[1] truly as I think, that it cannot be my duty to produce immediately in myself a feeling, such as sorrow when my opponent is humiliated or affection for a bore, though it might be my duty to do what I thought would encourage such feelings.

If then, as a determinist, I believed it impossible for me to do what I thought my duty, say to help a man though I more desired to hurt him, I should think I had a duty which I could not fulfil if I tried, desires not being immediately in my control. But the less I thought about such duties, as about spilt milk, the better. If it were argued that by thinking more about them I might come to desire more to do them, we must reply that this only puts the difficulty farther back; I could only do the suggested duty of thinking about them if I desired to do it more than anything incompatible.[2] To say 'I believe I ought' would only mean 'I should be better if I necessarily had certain desires more strongly'.

It has even been suggested[3] that the belief in freedom is illusory, though it is one we are necessarily compelled to retain, and that consequently we must always think and act precisely as if we were really free. But if there are demonstrably false beliefs which, on the most careful consideration, remain indubitable, we are reduced to the sceptical conclusion that not even the most convincing *refutation* of freedom would be in the least veridical.

---

[1] e.g. Ross.   [2] Cf. Ch. IV, § 9.
[3] Kant, *Fundamental Principles of the Metaphysic of Morals*, iii. 2 (80) (Abbott's trans., p. 67); Plekhanov, *Fundamental Problems of Marxism*, (trans. by E. and C. Paul, p. 93) seems to have the same idea.

§ 5. When we insist on this absurdity of believing in a duty to do what we believe we cannot do, determinists[1] sometimes reply that what we have thus wrongly described is really the absurdity of believing in a duty to do something we believe we could not do *if we chose*, and they still maintain that belief in a duty is compatible with a belief in the impossibility of choosing to do it. I agree that if we neither *think* we have an obligation (nor *a fortiori* a duty) to do an act nor most desire to do it, we cannot choose to do it, since these are the only possible reasons for choice, though it may be our *real* duty.[2] All I contend is that if we are to think we have a duty to do something (namely to try to bring about a certain result), we must think we can make the effort even though we more desire not to. If I do not try to move my finger that can only be because I did not choose. What I actually choose or will at any moment (as distinct from resolving to do in the future or intending to bring about indirectly) I not only can but necessarily must do. The determinist position seems to be that I can think I have a duty to do something so long as I think I should necessarily do it should something (namely 'choice') occur in my mind whose occurrence or absence is necessarily determined by desire.[3]

§ 6. I suggest a similar answer to the question how we can have conflicting obligations since we cannot perform both. It is not an actual ('objective') obligation but only what I think to be my duty ('my putative duty') which presupposes the freedom to choose whether to do it. There is no remorse or censure for not fulfilling a duty of which one was unaware. I may be unable to choose to fulfil an obligation, even when it is my duty, if I am unaware of it or if I think I have a stronger obligation, unless I happen to desire most to do so. I may be under obligation (or even duty) to pay a man money,

[1] e.g. Moore, *Ethics*.   [2] Cf. Ch. II, § 8 and Ch. III, § 6.
[3] Cf. Ch. IV, §§ 8, 9. In that context for 'choice' read 'reflection'.

but if I am unaware of the obligation, or think I have a stronger one to give the money in charity, and do not most desire to give it to him, I cannot choose to pay. But we should not say a man had an obligation to do what he could not do if he tried, as to be in two places at once or to stop his toothache. Nor could a man think it his duty to do what he thought he either could not do if he chose or could not choose to do. If he has no conflicting desire he must fulfil what he thinks his strongest obligation; if he thinks he has no obligation he must fulfil his strongest desire; between what he thinks his strongest obligation and a conflicting desire choice is free.

§ 7. I can myself see no improbability in a peculiar being like man, who is both rational and appetitive, being able to choose in which way he shall act when he thinks one course is his duty and desire solicits him to another. In thinking, our results are determined indeed, but partly by the facts we are attending to and partly by our capacity for understanding them, not wholly by our desires or we should reach none but wishful conclusions.[1] In thinking about conduct our beliefs as to the situation are similarly determined and so are our beliefs as to our consequent obligations, and our desires are determined in other ways. The alternatives, then, between which we choose are both determined, but I hold that our choice between them is free. Such freedom of such a being seems as intelligible as the causally determined behaviour of any other.[2] Whichever course a man chooses he can give an intelligible account of it: 'I took it because I wanted it', 'I left it because I thought I ought'.

---

[1] Cf. Hume, *Treatise*, I. iv. I: 'Reason must be considered as a kind of cause of which truth is one natural effect; but such a one as, by the irruption of other causes, and by the inconstancy of our mental powers, may frequently be prevented.'

[2] Hume and others who have denied the intelligibility of freedom have also denied that of causation (ibid. I. iii. 14 and II. iii. I). I do not know if they thought chance more intelligible.

§ 8. This brings us to the second determinist argument, the empirical one, that in fact we predict with some surety our own and other people's conduct, even from our limited knowledge of their character, and presumably could do so with certainty if that knowledge were complete. We know a good deal about a friend's tastes and moral beliefs, which are all determined by his innate temperament and intellectual capacity and by his past history. If we knew all about these facts we should know what in any situation he would most want to do and what he would think his duty. We might be able to say: 'He would think it wrong to kill a man for his rations and he would not want to unless perhaps he were mad with hunger', or 'He would never be a martyr for a religious dogma', but I think we could never tell whether on a given occasion he would do what he thought his duty or what he more desired. Similarly I am pretty sure there are some crimes I should not want to commit, and many things I should desire to do and not think wrong; so in these respects I am confident how I should behave. If there are men so holy that they never would desire anything so much as to do their duty they cannot be called free any more than God can,[1] who is presumed to be without desires, or than creatures who do not think they have any obligations.

§ 9. It may be argued that one of our strongest proclivities arises from habit, so that a man who had habitually chosen to do his duty would be determined so to choose again, and conversely one who has habitually chosen to follow his desires will not resist a new temptation. Obviously a man who has formed the habit of early rising will be less tempted in a similar situation to lie very long; he may even come to dislike it, and if he both prefers to rise and thinks it his duty he has no choice. I am not clear that this would tend to determine him to fulfil other duties, such as to keep his bed under doctor's orders, or to conceal his irritation when breakfast

[1] Kant: 'the holy will'.

was late. Ascetics are not always tolerant, nor the just kind.

The real puzzle here is how, if all choices between desire and duty are free they can be 'more difficult' when the desire is strong and the strongest obligation weak or very doubtful. I do not know the answer, but I should find it just as hard to say how, if all our choices are determined, they could ever be 'difficult' at all, for the 'difficulty' of choosing to do our duty when we would rather not is quite different from that of deciding which of two desires to gratify when they are equally strong.

§ 10. I have left to the last one argument in favour of determinism which I do not know how to deal with because I think it involves a general logical or metaphysical difficulty which I do not understand, though, perhaps for that reason, it is an argument which does not shake my conviction. This is the argument from averages: roughly the same number of actions of a given kind, say suicides, occur every year, or if the number varies much, causes such as bad weather or hard times can be ascribed. If such acts were free, it is said, we should not expect the total to be even so nearly predictable, yet we are prepared to invest our money with insurance companies on the actuarial calculations. I can only repeat that since desires and beliefs are certainly determined by factors whose changes can be roughly forecast we may know roughly how many people will want to commit suicide or not, and how strongly they will desire to do either, and how many will think it their duty or the reverse, and how strong they will think the obligation. Those whose desires and putative duties coincide will have no choice. When choices between two alternatives are free I see no reason for expecting them to be made either in equal or unequal numbers on the two sides.

But granting that we do expect statistical averages to be maintained under the same conditions, it would be a dubious inference that the individual acts we cannot predict are determined, since in the analogous case of the electrons the opposite conclusion has been drawn.

§ 11. My view, then, is that whenever any moral issue is raised, and only then, our action is free; and consequently such voluntary actions, which I think should alone be strictly called actions, have no motive in the proper sense of a desire which compels to either choice. We may be said to have two 'incentives' or 'grounds', our belief in an obligation and a contrary desire, between which we choose, and the one chosen is loosely called our motive. If we speak thus, we may say, rather absurdly, that we have 'made it our motive' by adopting it.[1]

My reason for this conclusion is my conviction that when I obey or disobey my conscience I could have chosen otherwise, and that I could not blame myself for disobeying it when it was contrary to desire if I thought I were determined to follow the strongest desire.

---

[1] Kant uses the phrase *selbst-bewirktes*.

XIII

SUMMARY

§ 1. RATIONAL beings take it for granted that they have the capacity for improving some states or activities of conscious beings and often also that they have entered into undertakings with other rational beings which they have the capacity to fulfil. If they reflect on these assumptions they conclude that they have obligations differing in degree, and perhaps conflicting, to do all these things, and that their duty is to fulfil the strongest, and that they can do this if they choose. Yet on further reflection they realize that none of these assumptions is certainly true, though the conclusion drawn from them is formally correct. What is true is that they can do what they think their duty, which is to try to affect in a certain way what they believe to be the present or future states or activities of other sentient beings. They may not only have mistaken the situation and the way it will naturally develop and their own capacities, but also they may have either through 'superstition' taken it for granted that they have obligations which further reflection convinces them they have not, or through obtuseness, overlooked obligations which they have.

Moreover, the formally correct conclusion is only clearly drawn where rationality is sufficiently developed for the necessary reflection to occur; some savages seem only to acknowledge obligations to fellow tribesmen; doubtless some types of obligation are still universally unsuspected. An obligation acknowledged pretty late in human history, hardly perhaps before the time of Socrates, was that of self-criticism, the refusal to take superstitions for granted or to assume that there were no more obligations to learn.

§ 2. Here arises a difficulty which I think the most fundamental of moral theory, but which I hardly find mentioned, even by those who are anxious to deny the reality of obligations, except by Hume. Why do we say that animals, infants, and some lunatics have no obligations? It cannot be because they do not recognize them, since nothing *could* be recognized which did not exist; nor yet because they do not believe in them, since belief is fallible; we think we all have objective obligations of which we are unaware, otherwise we could not say 'You are wrong, you really ought to do it', or 'You ought to do it if the situation is as you suppose'. Is it then because animals are incapable of freely choosing? But that which precludes them from freedom is the fact that they do not think they have any obligations, or rather do not conceive of obligation at all and therefore necessarily follow their strongest desire.

It is intelligible that only rational beings should be obliged to keep their undertakings since they alone can make them; it is also intelligible that they alone should think themselves obliged to inquire into the situation and their capacity for changing it and to reflect on the obligations involved, since they alone are capable of such inquiry and reflection and there can be no obligation to do what one could not do if one chose. But about the obligations of beneficence and improvement the question is more puzzling. Three answers seem possible: first, that there are no obligations other than putative, that is none that are real; second, that animals and infants have objective obligations, but that since they are totally unaware of them they cannot be praised or blamed; third, that objective obligations do actually come into existence together with rationality. My reasons for rejecting the first answer have been plain throughout.[1] I will only repeat here that I have never been persuaded that anybody is convinced by it; and I venture to agree with the greatest of sceptics[2] in an indifference to philosophical theories which, even if they admitted of no refutation, would carry no conviction. If the second answer were adopted, the difficulty

---

[1] Especially in Ch. II. [2] Hume.

would only recur a stage farther back, for why then should we deny that vegetables and bullets also have objective obligations? If a robin really ought not to kill its parent, ought a sapling to stifle its parent tree? If an infant has obligations, why not a germ-plasm? The third alternative then remains.

Since men were once infants and mankind has presumably been evolved from animals, it would seem that as we became rational we became obliged and more obliged as we became more rational; that with the senility of the individual and the race obligations must decay; and that when we fall asleep they lapse into the night of not being.

I can only commend this question, like some others, to more serious consideration than it has received, in the hopes of a more satisfactory answer.

NOTE. In an article on 'Freedom and Necessity' published in *Polemic* for Sept.–Oct. 1946, since this chapter was written, Professor Ayer maintains that freedom and causal determination are not incompatible. His argument is that causal determination is not the same as compulsion or constraint and therefore does not exclude freedom but only unpredictability. 'To say that I could have acted otherwise is to say (1) that I should have acted otherwise if I had chosen; (2) that my action was voluntary in the sense in which the actions, say, of the kleptomaniac are not; and (3) that nobody compelled me to act as I did.' But as to (1) the question is: Could I have *chosen* otherwise? As to (3) this is political or social freedom not freedom of the will. As to (2) 'the sense in which a kleptomaniac is not free' is that either he does not deliberate or his deliberation does not give him an alternative. Yet Professor Ayer admits that even deliberate action is deducible. By a free act he only means one not constrained by other persons but determined by a chain of causes one link in which was deliberation, itself determined. (Cf. Ch. IV, §§ 8, 9 above.)

PART II

POLITICAL THINKING

XIV

MORALS AND POLITICS[1]

§ 1. I HAVE now tried to outline the development of my own thinking about morals, a process conditioned, of course, partly by reading, but much more by the many hours which I have spent in discussing such topics with my pupils and colleagues. It seems a fair inference then that this development is much like that of other students, at least in its weighing of difficulties if not always in the final balance, which is indeed on a razor's edge.

It remains to indicate the bearing of my conclusions on some allied questions concerned either with 'applied ethics', that is the specification of the general principles, or with the relation of these moral principles to other subjects with which they are sometimes confused.

i. *The Ground of Allegiance*

Under the first heading there fall to be considered the moral foundations and the casuistry of political obligations. It seems often to be assumed that this subject comes under my second head, being not a specification or application of ethics but a different though cognate species of philosophy.

This view is suggested alike by popular sneers such as 'politics is a dirty business' and by oracular philosophisms on the unreality of individuals, with their claims and counter-

---

[1] See also my book with that title, where some of the topics here touched were treated in greater historical detail, though my own views were then somewhat different.

claims,[1] as compared with the state; and it has been encouraged by the traditional phrase, 'Morals *and* Politics'. But there is as much dirty business in the divorce courts and the stock-market as in politics; and without individuals and their counter-claims it is hard to see what the state would be or do. Politics are neither a trick below the notice of conscience nor a kingdom of heaven where morality has vanished into good nature.[2] They are a set of relations in which, as in any other, it is possible to do one's duty or to grind one's axe.

The issue has been further confused by another traditional phrase which asks: 'What is the End of the State?' I can only interpret this as meaning either: 'At what do people aim who, as statesmen or voters, have political power?' or 'At what ought they to aim?' The answer to the first question is historical: 'Sometimes at one thing, sometimes at another: —power, wealth, safety, for themselves or their country, the happiness of the world, justice, revenge, the spread of a religion.' The second question is a purely moral one. The idea that it is not has arisen, I think, from the relations of politics with law which is indeed distinguishable from obligation.

§ 2. One pressing question for the citizen or subject of a state is why or whether or when he ought to obey its laws, of which he may not approve; and though perhaps few to-day would identify morality with legality, we are all of us apt to accept as right laws and customs long established, at least so long as they fit our private convenience; and there is some obligation to respect them even when they are not right. But another question which every ruler and every enfranchised

---

[1] Bosanquet, *Value and Destiny of the Individual*, v; cf. Hegel on 'mere morality' as subordinate to tradition and institution, *Philosophie des Rechts* (trans. Knox), § 260, and elsewhere and *Philosophie der Geschichte* (trans. Sibree), Introduction. Cf. Burke, *Reflections on the French Revolution*, and Mussolini, speech on 'International Conciliation', January 1935, and 'Charter of Labour' (*Gazetta Officiale*, C. I (30.iv.27)).

[2] *Sittlichkeit*; cf. the Marxian Utopia where all conflict will cease.

citizen *ought* to ask himself is what laws and what customs should rightly be abolished and what retained, what obeyed and what resisted; and I do not see how this question could be answered except in terms of his obligations to his fellow men, which I have argued can be roughly specified as beneficence,[1] improvement, and justice. Some writers, however, have identified political obligation with one only of these, and some have exalted it above all three, and indeed above obligation to our fellows altogether, as an inspiration of the National Spirit which they call the General Will, something not our reason which makes for righteousness, or at least for the glories of our blood and state.

§ 3. The General Will is not identified with the actual wills of a majority or even with the political blue moon of unanimity; it is always right, at least in its aim if not in its technique; its aim is not internal or external justice, which belongs to 'the unreal world of claims and counter-claims', where interests differ, but 'the Common Good' of the citizens which they may quite ignore since their actual wills are for their private good. It is in fact a 'Hidden Hand' shaping men's selfish ends to a divine event; it is the manifestation of an immanent and universal Reason or of an economic necessity; it is what an earlier age, unashamed of naked theology, called the Will of God, which was often identified with the Divine Right of the Lord's Annointed,[2] or by a later age, unashamed of naked materialism, with the Dictatorship of the Proletariat. But it is in vain that this blessed name of General Will has been taken by either reactionaries or revolutionists; for it is vain to enlist our hard efforts, and especially

---

[1] Including or as well as the increase of liberty.

[2] I am summarizing what I understand of Rousseau's *Contrat Social*, Burke's 'divine tactic', Hegel's 'Cunning of the Idea', Bosanquet's 'real will', and some of Mussolini's speeches which I conjecture to have been inspired if not written by the neo-Hegelian Gentile, and which, translated into English, would surely be ascribed to Burke. Cf. also the exponents of Dialectical Materialism and the Economic Interpretation of History.

our hard thinking, on behalf of an end already predetermined. If there is anything we can do about politics at all, there must be obligations, to be sought by reason, in the way of justice, beneficence, or improvement for our fellows. That might is right, or a sign of right, is a doctrine which was reduced to absurdity before it had been fully developed: if all powers that be have a claim on our obedience, then a common constable, a Borgia, or even a bandit chieftain may have as good claim as any sovereign or constitution—until the times do alter.[1]

As I can form no idea of wills which are not the wills of rational beings, nor even of desires which are not the desires of sentient beings, and as there appears no evidence what such wills will, or how many there are, or whether they exist, I shall leave this attempt to put political behaviour above or below the sphere of morality and turn to the two views which severally make it a department either of justice or of beneficence.

§ 4. The last alternative must of course be taken by all who hold the utilitarian theory of morals. But all the arguments I have urged against that theory apply. The only reason for holding that in our political actions we need not consider a just distribution of opportunities for happiness or improvement, but only the increase of the total amount, would be that by our moral theory we were committed to the doctrine that there can be no other duty than the latter. So far as utilitarians neglect justice and individual rights and look solely to a totality of good results, they should logically, however reluctant, look with favour on a totalitarian policy. A theory, on the other hand, which admits conflicting claims and obligations, and consequently the frequent duty of compromise, seems more consistent with democratic institutions that respect minority rights.

§ 5. The other view, that every political duty, or at least the most widespread one of obedience to the laws, is based

---

[1] Summarized from Hume, *Essay on the Original Contract.*

solely upon the justice of contract-keeping, does not seem
derived from any general theory of ethics. It would be more
superficially attractive if it also covered the other political
duty of good government and legislation, but in earlier times
political philosophies were mainly constructed by members
or adherents of a governing class who were more interested
in obedience than in good government. Partly for this reason
the contract was usually supposed made not between subjects and rulers, but between prospective subjects, so that
the sovereign, being no party to it, was not bound by its
terms.[1] Nor does the other reason for supposing a contract,
the alleged peculiarity of the obligation to obey laws we do
not approve, seem to apply to the duties of good legislation,
administration, or foreign policy.

The obvious and I think fatal objection to the contractual
theory of allegiance is that no such origins of government
are recorded, and we know that many governments, with as
good claims as any others to obedience, had a very different
history. If we believed that such a contract had been made
by our remote forefathers we should want to know its terms,
whether of absolute or conditional obedience,[2] and we should
also ask whether they could bind their descendants or citizens
of other origin in perpetuity. We have a similar obligation
to obey some commands of our parents which we may not
think very wise, but it is not suggested that we contracted
with our infant brothers and sisters to do so, or even that our
god-parents promised one another in our names. If it be
urged that the contract is not historical but only a 'logical
analysis' of our allegiance, this only means that we ought to

---

[1] Hobbes's *Leviathan*. All that is of value in Hobbes's contract theory
might be retained by abandoning his hedonistic psychology and admitting
utilitarian and even agathistic motives for making and keeping the contract. In fact he sometimes implies this (Chs. XIII and XVII *ad fin.*).

[2] Locke (*Essay on Civil Government*) thought government is fiduciary.
The prospective subjects agree to hand it over to the sovereign as a
revocable trust. Rousseau envisages such a trust to the executive.

obey 'just as if' we had contracted to do so. Such an 'analysis' might as fairly be applied to our duties of beneficence—we ought to spare pain just as if we had promised. The assumption is that all duties are ultimately contractual; an explicit promise would be otiose.

§ 6. In face of these difficulties a tacit has usually been substituted for an explicit contract. By living in a country, by using the roads and public services, by accepting the protection of police, especially if we have inherited property, we are supposed to be pledged to obedience. It is therefore with those recently possessing power and not with any rightful claimant to it such as an oppressed majority that the tacit agreement is presumed; nor does it appear that a man with no 'stake in the country' and few legal rights, who could have bettered himself by emigration had he been able and permitted, is governed by such consent. Accordingly some supporters of the tacit contract apply it only or eminently to democracies. They argue that, as by tossing up, so by voting, one implicitly agrees to abide by the result. But the cases are very different. One may know beforehand that he will be in a minority, yet he cannot stand out: but nobody would agree to abide by the toss if an adverse result were pretty certain. The mugwump by refusing to vote does not become a chartered libertine. The fact is we are born into a state, not contracted. It is just in this point that citizenship differs from voluntary associations which I freely join and can quit when they cease to serve my selfish or benevolent purposes.

§ 7. Even the utilitarian view would come nearer describing my attitude to the law. The obligation I feel to obey enactments not to my interest and which I do not approve depends upon the probable effects of doing so, not upon the past unless I have accepted a position of trust or taken an oath of allegiance. Governments which use arguments or propaganda to their subjects say very little about contract; if they have no case for some particular law they claim loyal obedience on the ground of their general indispensability as the only safeguard of security and prosperity; they appeal to the past only as evidence of their future conduct; and in all this they seem to be wise. Every law is part of a system of law or of a constitution, and open defiance of one law is apt to weaken respect for the whole.

§ 8. It is noteworthy that the quite secret evasion of a law we disapprove, e.g. of total prohibition by drinking an old private cellar, would be slightly blamed in comparison with a black-market traffic which encourages the bootleg and the gangster. Even such secret disobedience is sometimes condemned on the ground that I ought not to do an act in itself innocuous if similar actions done by many people would have a bad effect: in idiomatic language, 'I ought to play the game'.[1] If we think that a system of government on the whole has the will and the power to secure more justice, more happiness, and more improvement in the world than any which we are likely to put in its place without causing more injustice, misery, and degeneration in the process, then we ought to do nothing likely to weaken it, or at least we have a strong obligation against doing so. This provision of justice, happiness (including liberty), and improvement, I take to be the ground of allegiance. The obligation to obedience needs no general will and no contract; it can be analysed entirely in terms of obligations to our fellow men, and it covers all those obligations, not any one only. It is also the 'end of the State', the purpose which all who have any share in government whether as voters or legislators *ought* to pursue. One of the obligations of a representative or executive may arise from a contract, overt or implied, into which he has entered with those who appointed him, and a judge may sometimes have to weigh incompatible obligations to administer justice or the law; but I do not think my duty as a subject or a voter is much affected by contractual considerations.

[1] See Ch. IX, § 13.

§ 9. Even if the tacit contract of obedience be watered down into gratitude for benefits received,[1] it is evident that the fellow countrymen by whose labours I profit are mostly dead; that most of those whom I can politically benefit are infants or unborn, and that in some cases I might benefit them most by revolution. It is never suggested that my duty to my children depends upon gratitude to my parents or upon a contract to hand on precisely the education I was given.

ii. *The Ideal State*

§ 10. Political philosophers have spent much effort on determining the best form of state, which in the formula I have adopted should mean the constitution most likely to effect the happiness and improvement of mankind and to distribute these benefits justly. This formula really agrees with the old conclusion[2] that for any constitutional device— monarchy, oligarchy, democracy—there may be a good form which aims at the public good, or, as I should prefer to say, at a just distribution of as much happiness and goodness as possible, and a bad form which aims only at the advantage of the rulers whether a king, an oligarchy, or a majority. 'The form that is *most justly* administered is best.'

In our time and country, the most interesting form of the question is how to justify our conviction that democracy is the kind of constitution most likely to take this good form, and therefore to have the strongest claim to our loyalty, though a majority may be as unjust and is often less clever and efficient than other rulers.

Those who discuss this topic to-day in 'brains trusts' and other places where they talk commonly seem to confuse three questions: one is 'What is the usual meaning of the term democracy, common to those who like the thing and those who do not?'; another is: 'What are the advantages and disadvantages of this arrangement, or is it perhaps an end in

---

[1] Ibid., § 9.   [2] Aristotle, *Politics*, III. vii.

itself which we ought to aim at for its own sake irrespective of such considerations?'; and the third is: 'With what other good devices should democratic institutions be combined so as to work successfully and secure their end (if they have an end beyond themselves) and to deserve our allegiance?' The answer to the first question is, I suppose: 'The word democracy is commonly used and understood to mean a government of the whole people by the majority, generally through representatives, elected nowadays by a secret ballot of the adult population.' Lincoln's eloquent aphorism of course will not do. Democracy is government of the whole people by a majority and it may be carried out either for the whole people or merely for the majority without consideration of minority rights. The answer to the second and third questions I shall now proceed to discuss, only premising that, like every constitutional device, democracy can be wielded for the purely selfish interest of the rulers, but cannot deserve our allegiance unless it is disinterested,[1] or at least behaves as if it were.

§ 11. To many of the ancients it appeared a truism that the best form of government is government by the best men rather than by the majority. Indeed, if we had a prescription for discovering an incorruptibly perfect goodness and wisdom in any man or set of men, we should as readily commit ourselves to their guidance as to the will of God, since one result of such wisdom and goodness would be a proper economy in the exercise of power, so that a degree of political freedom would be devolved upon the subjects analogous to the moral freedom thought to be allowed by a divine creator to mankind.[2]

But this is Utopian. There is no infallible selection of the wise or good, not birth, nor wealth, nor civil service examina-

---

[1] I suppose it is majority tyranny that Burke had in mind when he said 'A perfect democracy is the most shameless thing in the world' (*French Revolution*).

[2] The analogy seems suggested by Milton, see Saurat, *Milton, Man and Thinker*, and cf. 'Whose service is perfect freedom'.

tions, nor psychological tests, least of all testimonials; the selectors are fallible, we are reduced to trial and error. Even if we could appoint a superman our dictator, we know that human nature, exempt from criticisms, opposition, and compromise, would be overwrought; for 'Power tends to corrupt and absolute power corrupts absolutely. Great men are nearly always bad men.'[1] Children with only one living parent are generally better at boarding-school, for the differences between the parents, when conducted with good temper, are the salvation of themselves and their children, of themselves from the conceit of infallibility, and of their children from monotheistic idolatry. Absolute monarchy by 'the best man' in practice exemplifies the adage that the best ideals work worst;[2] oligarchy is better, for the oligarchs at least quarrel and criticize one another.

§ 12. The ancient condemnations of democracy were partly due to the fact that the word then had a different meaning; it meant not government by majority-elected representatives but a universal chance of office,[3] so far as possible by rotation, or, if the jobs would not go round, by lot, a device which worked as badly as might be expected. Election of representatives is a kind of retrievable trial and error for securing what the ancients meant by aristocracy or constitutional government. Whether the few are wiser (or taller) than the many depends on where the line is drawn; nothing prevents a majority from containing all or some of the wisest nor a minority most of the fools. In one point the many are always wiser than the few; they know what shoe pinches most feet, and will at least try to choose good cobblers. We do not let cooks choose our dinners, since the proof of the pudding is in the eating.

[1] Lord Acton. The thought is Greek. Responsible power *proves* men.
[2] *Corruptio optimi pessima.*
[3] Aristotle, *Politics*, III. iv, VII. ii. This device survives in this country only in the appointment of juries by lot and of a few municipal officers by rotation.

§ 13. Contrary to a received opinion, I think democracy is more desirable, even if more cumbrous, in a large than in a small community, especially if its administration be decentralized. Even an absolute ruler is seldom so inhuman as to be very brutal to his immediate neighbours and acquaintances, but sympathy with twenty million unfranchised subjects is watery; domestic slavery was seldom so bad as in the great plantations; in a very small community, moreover, the choice of able governors is restricted and apt to be hampered by the jealousy of neighbours and old school-fellows.

Further, since majority rule offers obvious incentives to proselytism, it tends to displace coercion by persuasion, and so to foster habits of conciliation and the love of peace; it counts heads instead of breaking them, and the heads you count are those you have persuaded.

But the decisive advantage of a majority as against all oligarchies is that it is a fluctuating power; you may have the Voice of the People with you to-day on one point, but I shall have it to-morrow on another, so neither of us is apt to press it intolerantly as the Voice of God.

Where the division between majority and minority is relatively permanent, as in cases of a ruling race or caste, entailed wealth, or religious sects, this great advantage vanishes. If the barrier cannot be broken down there seems to be a strong claim for secession.[1]

§ 14. These are the main grounds on which I think that a democracy generally has a better claim on our allegiance and our submission, even to its follies when resistance would weaken it, than any other form of government; it is a better device for effecting what we ought to try to effect. But it is not knave-proof, and I should think some other form which allowed freedom of speech and criticism and organization better than a democracy which denied these to a minority. I think it prudent in a democracy to pay an opposition and

[1] See Ch. XVI, § 3.

gallant to tolerate conscientious objectors. Party government, like every other, if selfishly worked, is bad, but it is less likely than a one-party state to be worked quite selfishly. Its possibility demands a good deal of intelligence, and intelligence therefore is one of the things any government ought to promote.[1]

The reasons I have given for preferring democracy or majority government to other forms are in a loose sense 'utilitarian'; they treat it as a device which we ought to adopt and maintain not for its own sake but for its results, though among the results for which we ought to adopt it is justice, which we have an obligation to promote for its own sake and not only so far as it increases general happiness, which last alone gives justice any value for utilitarians.

§ 15. Democracy is, however, sometimes defended as a method of organization which we have some obligation to adopt for its own sake. It is said that every man has a natural right to a voice or vote on the way he should be governed, which seems to imply that the others have a stronger obligation to obey a cruel and oppressive majority than a good government of any other kind. This seems to me very dubious; at least an ignorant or selfish man could only have a *claim* to such voice, which would be overridden by the claims of other people not to be endangered by it. What seems true is that every man has a claim to such improvement, in the way of education and training, as might fit him to exercise such a voice justly and beneficially. There is an obligation then on any undemocratic government, say a paternal ruler over less civilized peoples, to fit them to become self-governing, and this is analogous to a strong obligation of parents to their children.

[1] Collingwood, *The New Leviathan*, pp. 226–7.

XV

THE RIGHTS OF MAN[1]

i. *Equality*

§ 1. DEMOCRACY may no doubt be defended on utilitarian grounds since even a tyrannical majority aims at the happiness of the greater number though not necessarily at the greatest total amount, nor necessarily counting every man as one, if that means endeavouring to distribute happiness equally or fairly. I think its more indisputable claim to be the best form of government is as being most likely to defend the rights of the individual.

Life, liberty (including freedom of speech and 'freedom of conscience'), 'property', and the pursuit of happiness have commonly been enumerated as natural rights and so sometimes have the right to vote and the right to work. Against the utilitarian view that our only political duty can be to increase happiness it has been maintained that it is to defend such rights.

As was said before, natural rights have been prejudiced by the attempt to give a list of them as 'inalienable'.[2] But every right, like its corresponding duty, depends upon the situation; it is natural as being no fiction but something naturally arising out of that situation, and inalienable so long, but only so long, as that situation does not relevantly change. This prejudicial language may be excused by the need for rebutting the suggestion that 'rights are made by recognition'.[3] What is recognized must already exist. If the absurd phrase means that rights cannot be respected till they

---

[1] Cf. Ch. V.

[2] Locke, *Essay on Civil Government*; Paine, *The Rights of Man*; and more emphatically Jefferson, *The Declaration of Independence* (U.S.A.), and the *Declaration of the Rights of Man* (French National Assembly).

[3] T. H. Green, *Political Obligation*, § 136. Cf. Austin, *Lectures on Jurisprudence*, vi.

are recognized it is a platitude; if it be more significantly interpreted as meaning that every man has a right only to what it is generally recognized to be for the 'common good' that he should have,[1] this would imply that the majority can do no wrong. But if, as I maintain, we have obligations of justice towards individuals as well as to improve and benefit mankind in general, then those to whom we have these objective obligations must have just claims that they should be fulfilled, and the strongest obligation in any situation will constitute a duty, to which must correspond a right on their part whether recognized or not. Duties and the corresponding rights cannot be willed, nor can they objectively depend upon anybody's opinion about them; subjectively speaking, my duties would depend upon my beliefs about the situation and your rights upon yours; putatively they would depend severally upon our several opinions about what the situation, as each of us supposes it to be, morally demands.[2]

§ 2. The mistake has been to speak of natural rights, which would be absolute, rather than of natural claims, which might conflict so that only the strongest would be a right; and also to call them inalienable, which would seem to make them not depend upon the situation. If every man had a right to life, no criminal might ever be killed either in self-defence or to prevent a massacre; no man might be compelled to risk his life in any cause; every member of a starving group would have a right to the subsistence rations which were not obtainable, and every patient to a full dose of penicillin; it could never be our painful duty to let one man die to save a thousand. And all such difficulties apply yet more clearly to the alleged rights of liberty, of possessions, of improvement, and of the means to happiness. Thought is no doubt always free as it cannot be coerced, though it may be persuaded by argument or irrational propaganda and suppression of facts, and in most situations a man has a

[1] Green seems to hint at this interpretation.   [2] See Ch. II.

claim not to be deceived. Conscience is always free if that means that a man can always do what he thinks he ought in the situation however circumscribed. If it is meant that a man should always be free to perform what he considers religious duties, which might include human sacrifice, the extermination of heretics, or the destruction of unorthodox literature, such a claim is easily overridden. Freedom to affect others as conscience may dictate must always, like all freedoms, be limited by other claims and especially by the claims of others to a like amount of freedom. If one man had complete freedom to do as he chose, he would probably leave little to the rest. Men could only have a right to *equal* freedom, as they could only have a right to equal means of subsistence. Indeed, equality of consideration is the only thing to the whole of which men have a right.

The value of democracy resides then chiefly, as I think, in the fact that it seems the most probable means of securing to every individual equality of consideration, which involves that it would secure him a fair share of all those things to which he has, as a man, natural claims. First would come freedom, the power of doing what he chooses without co-ercion or intimidation; and since he would certainly choose to have the means of happiness, including possessions, and the power freely to speak his mind, it implies all the so-called natural and inalienable rights of man. Perhaps freedom of speech is the only natural claim which is always a right, for it is difficult to see how one man by talking and writing can prevent others from doing so or from doing anything whatever. If they were compelled to come to his lecture or read his books, that, of course, would be a different story.[1]

§ 3. The most fundamental natural right, then, is to equality; but equality itself must be defined by the situation. It does not imply the same ration for an infant and a heavy

---

[1] See § 14 below.

worker, nor the same education for a genius and a fool, nor the same amenities for a criminal and a hero. The Greek formula 'equals to equals'[1] as a description of justice[2] requires to be qualified as 'equal treatment of those who are equal in relevant respects'. It is just to treat men as equal until some reason, other than preference, such as need, capacity, or desert, has been shown to the contrary.

§ 4. There does seem to be some fundamental and constant respect in which men are equal, equally set above the sentient animals, as well as the vegetable and lifeless world; capable of morality, of affection, of degrees and kinds of happiness and misery peculiar to their species; 'how noble in reason, how infinite in faculty,—in apprehension how like a god, the beauty of the world'.[3] This, I think, was what was meant by the dark saying that we should treat all rational beings as ends, never as means only, and by the unexpected inference that this implied making their ends, among which would always be their happiness, our own.[4]

§ 5. It is also, I think, fair to commend equality ethically on purely utilitarian grounds, since the pain of approaching the subsistence level is greater than the pleasure of luxury, and it is also likely that irritation at one's own inferior treatment is greater than the pleasant pride of superiority. Against this last point has been instanced the gloating of many poor and humble over the extravagance of the wild rich. But such romantic sentimentality need not be taken very seriously. Most housewives who revel in the fashion-gossip of society papers would more gladly read of a rise in their husbands' wages, as girls who vicariously luxuriate in the thwarted passions of high life often accept a good offer of marriage.

---

[1] ἴσα τοῖς ἴσοις, i.e. *ceteris paribus*; or κατ' ἀξίαν (in accordance with desert), Aristotle, *Eth. Nic.* 1158^{b}30.

[2] Ibid. 1129^{b}34. Cf. Ch. VII, § 1.

[3] Shakespeare, *Hamlet*, II. ii.

[4] Kant, *Grundlegung*, trans. by Abbott, *Fundamental Principles of the Metaphysic of Morals*, ii.

Perhaps the strongest evidence that there is a fundamental belief in the obligation to treat men equally or fairly is the almost universal doctrine that all men are equal in the sight of God, who is no respecter of persons, and that the inequality of their states below is a result of or a concession to their wickedness.

ii. *Liberty*[1]

§ 6. Among the things men claim, after equality comes liberty. Equality must come first as the condition of all others because, as has been said, it is only to an equal or fair share of available goods that a man can have a right, and only to as much liberty as does not interfere with the like liberty of others.[2] Liberty must come next because so far as a man has liberty to do what he likes he will be able to get most of the things he wants, including those to which he has claims. What most men want most is life, which can only be destroyed against their will by violent infraction of their liberty.

§ 7. The words 'liberty' and 'freedom', which I do not distinguish, are sometimes used with qualifying phrases such as 'freedom from disease', 'free from rain', but when used absolutely they always mean social freedom, which I define as 'the power of doing what one would choose unaffected by the action (coercion or intimidation) of other *persons*'. The only exceptions to this usage is, I think, in what may be called the philosophical or moral sense of freedom of choice,[3] that

---

[1] See Maitland, 'Liberty' (*Collected Papers*, i). See also my article in *Law Quarterly*, January 1940.

[2] Mill, *Liberty*. Or perhaps we should say that men have a claim to complete liberty nearly always overridden by the superior claims of others to an equal share or by different claims.

[3] See Ch. XII above. Moral and social freedom seem to be confused by Croce in his discussion of liberty, to the detriment of the argument. *Discorsi di varia filosofia*, especially xvii, 'Libertà e giustizia'. His reply to this criticism (*Quaderni della Critica*, March 1945) is that man is only free, either morally or politically, when he does his duty. This usage I cannot understand. It removes responsibility for wrong acts. No doubt it derives from Hegel. Cf. Ch. XII, § 1.

is, the capacity to choose undetermined by one's own past history, and with this we have at present no concern.

The words are sometimes, however, used in a narrower and I think improper, that is unusual, sense. Freedom is sometimes identified with what should be called *legal freedom*, that is to say the unimpeded power of doing what the law does not forbid,[1] as if it were impossible for laws themselves by enforcing slavery to diminish liberty; and in the same sense it has been identified with obedience to the laws of my state.[2] Perhaps by obedience here was meant willing obedience, but willing obedience to anybody, say to my pirate captain, is of course liberty. I do not think it is so common to mistake 'equality before the law', which may consist in legal serfdom, with equality.

§ 8. But the meaning of the word has also been narrowed in the opposite direction, so that men are called free in proportion as they are not restrained and protected by law from mutual oppression. Different travellers often bring strangely inconsistent reports of the amount of freedom enjoyed in some country with a social system unlike their own; those who look only at legal restriction may call it very unfree, but those who consider its legal prevention of the possibilities for private and economic oppression may call it the home of freedom. Perhaps it is because any wide distribution of freedom depends upon a strong constraint over potentially oppressive classes and individuals that constraint and freedom have been identified. But this is like identifying plenty with ration cards, which are only a device for securing an equal approach to it.

§ 9. A third and allied misuse of the word 'liberty' is to

---

[1] *Libertas est potestas faciendi id quod jure licet.*

[2] Hegel, *Philosophie des Rechts*, trans. by Knox, §§ 15, 140 (*e*), 206. But, slipping back to the usual meaning, he argued that this is always what I really want to do. Cf. Bradley, *Ethical Studies*, 'My Station and its Duties', and Bosanquet, *Philosophical Theory of the State*, pp. 107, 127.

confine it to the power of doing what we ought,[1] the power of doing other things being then dyslogistically called licence. It might be convenient to restrict 'liberty' to the power of doing what we choose so long as that does not impede the like liberty of others, and to call any individual freedom exceeding that 'licence'; but this is not the normal usage. There is already a name 'discipline' for the forcible equalization of liberty.

The prevention of both morally indifferent and criminal acts impairs the liberty of those who wish to do them. It would be monstrous to call me quite free if I were prevented by the police from smoking or even from oversmoking, though I do not claim that I have any obligation to do either. I think in our definition of liberty we ought to abandon all moral terms; otherwise we could not ask *how much* liberty children or weak-minded persons ought to have. It has indeed been asked: 'What crimes have not been committed in the *name* of freedom?' as if this implied a misnomer. But of course, no crime was ever committed when the criminal was unfree, through physical restraint or fear, to commit it, though most crimes diminish general liberty. It is not true that liberty is best beloved by best men, though other people's liberty may be; the old lag abandons hope on entering a life sentence, while a very good man might take a cage for a hermitage. Laws are always meant to restrict somebody's freedom and are good laws when, though not only when, they do this in order to secure a greater freedom for others. They succeed in this object when they are strictly and efficiently executed.

§ 10. By the definition offered the maximum interference with my liberty would be imprisonment in close manacles; a minimum the exclusion from one spot or locked safe which I wished to enter. The most free man would be one solitary on an island, who would certainly find his unchartered

[1] T. H. Green, *Political Obligation*.

freedom tiresome and gladly sacrifice it by coming under captain's orders, for while the unfree must be unhappy, the free may be more so. After him, most freedom is enjoyed by the quite irresponsible despot who, unlike the ship-wrecked sailor, very much diminishes the freedom of many other persons. As compared with a close prisoner, a slave always has much freedom in his hours of rest, and even at labour he can probably work left- or right-handed as he pleases; even a convict if unchained has a good deal; and, as with most of us, his freedom is less limited by stone walls and iron bars than by fear of them. If laws are disobeyed we may be merely fined, but if we do not pay we shall be haled to prison.

§ 11. I will now try to justify the terms of my definition, which was 'the power of doing what one would choose un-affected by the action (coercion or intimidation) of other persons'.

(1) *Doing*. (*a*) As I have said, our *thinking* cannot be con-strained, though it may be influenced by others in rational or irrational ways, such as argument, false propaganda, or suppression of facts and valid arguments. Silent thought is always free. (*b*) Our *feelings* can be painfully influenced by others when they smack us or whistle out of tune or, if we love them, by their indifference or neglect. If I want to read or to sleep, noises forced upon me diminish my freedom. The parent or lover is not free from anxiety, but he is (socially) free.

(2) *What one would choose*. If I am forbidden under penalty to do what I should not choose, for instance to bait bears on Sunday, or am prevented, for instance by fences, from walking over a cliff in the dark, my freedom is not im-paired. A penal law against murder only limits the freedom of would-be murderers. It might seem to follow that no law which a man obeys willingly, that is when he could escape detection, makes him less free. We often obey inconvenient

laws, by whose repeal we should choose to profit, either from a blind habit of law-abiding[1] or from the reflection that any known general law, however bad, interferes less with freedom than private war and scramble or arbitrary and unforeseen decisions, and that our disobedience might lead to such anarchy.[2] A slave or convict who refused emancipation because of habit and inertia must, I think, be called a free fool at least until he repents. The man who resists his desire to trespass on a deer-forest from reflective conscience and not from fear must be called free, and this applies to a hungry man who similarly would not steal when detection is impossible. The degree of detriment to my freedom depends upon the strength of the wish frustrated; a starving man prevented from taking food is less free than a smoker denied tobacco, so that laws safeguarding possessions diminish the freedom of the poor much more than that of the rich,[3] though a man may, on other grounds, have a claim to superior possessions which overrides the claim to arithmetical equality.

These considerations will lead us presently to a discussion of the next 'natural right', that of property.

(3) *Other persons.* I have given reasons for confining 'liberty' and 'freedom', when the words are not qualified, to the absence of restraint by other persons.[4] A man prevented from doing what he would otherwise choose by fear of the supernatural may not be free from superstition, but he is socially free.

[1] See Hume, *Essays*, I. iv, 'Antiquity always begets opinion of right.' When our conservative fear of instability through innovation conflicts with our reforming fear of oppression through obsolescence, Hume thinks anarchy the worse evil but oppression the more likely.

[2] The best reasoned defence of anarchy is Godwin's *Political Justice*, VII. viii, much modified, however, in VIII. ii.

[3] 'Whenever we depart from equality we rob the poor of more satisfaction than the rich' (Hume, *Enquiry*, iii) and 'Property when united causes more dependence [i.e. less freedom] than when dispersed' (*Essays*, I. vii).   [4] § 7 above.

Any persons may restrict my freedom, a neighbour, a dictator, a majority; and my having voted for the law makes no difference if I should now choose to break it but for fear. Ulysses' sailors impaired his freedom by his own orders when they prevented him from joining the Sirens. I can even limit my own freedom by locking myself in an upper story and throwing out the key, but not by vows or promises without enforceable penalty. I am free to break them.

(4) *Interference.* So far as our action is restricted not by other people's action but by their failure to act, I do not think we should say our freedom is impaired. To block my path seems to limit my freedom; failure to clear or repair it does not. But the distinction is difficult to draw: 'Thou shalt not kill, but need'st not strive Officiously to keep alive.' I suppose that if I fail to remove obstructions erected rightly or wrongfully on land I have inherited, I am rightly or wrongfully diminishing the freedom of those who rightly or wrongfully wish to pass. And if I do not try to remove economic and legal restrictions by which I profit, the same seems to hold good.

(5) *Action.* (*a*) I mean action here to include credible threat of action, which is the most usual diminution of liberty, but not deception or refusal of information. I think to drug a man or (if possible) to hypnotize him against his will would deprive him of freedom, but rhetorical or other emotional propaganda would not, though to forbid his access to contrary propaganda, if he wished to enjoy it, or to force him to listen to me, would.

(*b*) Bribes and promises, unlike threats and punishments, do not impair freedom. The man likes earning the bribe better than not being offered it, whereas the man moved by threats would have preferred to act otherwise could he have done so fearlessly.

§ 12. My definition, thus explained, seems to me the most consonant with the usage of the words 'freedom' and 'liberty'. It makes clear the following two points:

(*a*) There are other good things and other things to which men have claims besides liberty, which may conflict with it, such as those to education and security and hygiene;[1] Robinson Crusoe may have had a claim as well as a wish to be restored to the restraints of society.

(*b*) One man's liberty is apt to be inimical to his neighbour's and a man has a claim to equal liberty only, or to as much as does not impair the like liberty of others. Almost the only freedom which never does this is freedom of speech and writing when there is no compulsion on hearers or readers.[2]

It remains to ask how far equal liberty is favoured or endangered by other kinds of equality.

(1) I have argued that 'political equality' or democracy does not guarantee liberty any more than does minority government, but is generally more favourable to it.

(2) 'Equality before the law', if that means law effectively carried out and legally administered, is implied in the very notion of law, and almost any such system is preferable to anarchy or despotic edict. But it is questionable how far the laws regulating property in some communities make so well for the maximum of liberty as do, say, the laws against murder and assault. This leads to the subject of the next chapter, but a few points about liberty may first be mentioned.

§ 13. Liberty, like equality, can be defended on utilitarian grounds both as a constituent of happiness and as a means to it.[3] The argument would be that our duty is to increase

[1] A Sumerian king claims fame as having given his people 'equal justice and canals' (Woolley, *Abraham*). Cf. Burke, *Reflections on the French Revolution.*

[2] See § 14, below.

[3] J. S. Mill in *Liberty* mainly pleads for freedom of speech as the surest means to the attainment of useful truth and to progress, but he sometimes passes to the other argument and treats it as something to which men have equal claims for its own sake.

general happiness and improvement and that, since all men have a strong desire to be happy and some desire to be improved, this duty is generally best fulfilled by allowing the greatest amount of equal liberty. I am not sure whether it is more correct to say that every man has a claim to do whatever he would choose free from coercion and intimidation, but a claim which is generally overridden by the claims of other people not to be coerced and intimidated by him, or that no man has a claim to more than an equal amount of such freedom. In either case his claim may conflict with other claims and cannot therefore, as such, be 'absolute', but is 'inalienable'. The strongest of conflicting claims is a right, which is absolute, since there are no conflicting rights, but alienable if the situation alters. To either claim would correspond an obligation and to every right a duty.

§ 14. Freedom of speech is a claim perhaps less often overridden than any other. It is seldom overridden by the like claim of others, since my long-windedness, except in special circumstances of debate, shortens nobody else's, nor even by any claim to general liberty, since my lecture, when attention is not compulsory, prevents nobody from doing what he would choose. The only plausible exceptions appear to be 'careless talk', 'slander', and 'incitements to violence'. In general my own view would be that argument (as distinct from incitements) for intolerance should be tolerated as 'monuments of the safety with which error of opinion may be tolerated where reason is left free to combat it'.[1] Yet it seems paradoxical that we ought to allow arguments for persecution but resist persecution itself.

The distinction legally recognized between cool argument and incitement to violence is no doubt often very hard to draw, but seems even more necessary to the moralist than to the lawyer. To argue that since a man extremely diminishes the freedom of many others he ought to be forcibly pre-

---

[1] Ascribed to Jefferson; I do not know the reference.

vented is to argue, rightly or wrongly, in favour of general liberty. To incite violence against anybody by false accusations, or by emotional stimulus which cannot claim to be 'true', is certainly wrong and does appear to be an *attempt* to infringe *his* liberty though not that of the dupes.

iii. *Property*[1]

§ 15. It seems otiose to speak of the right to property, for we mean by property those physical things which a man has a right to use. I can hardly think of anything which a man has the right to use in any way he chooses; I may not fire my gun in the high street; I may not use my money for bribery, nor even my hands for assault or larceny. Whether or when we have a right to transfer property will need to be discussed. I do not think the word is usually applied to things not physical, which I might in a sense 'possess' and 'use', such as skill, information, reputation, affection, good looks. We do not even call a man's life his property. The right to services is not called property, unless we think that a man can have a right to slaves. Whether the name should be applied to benefices, royalties, patents, copyrights, is arguable; if it is the profits or emoluments that are in question, these, I suppose, in the long run are rights to control physical things; if it is anything else, I suppose it must be reputation.

That there is such a thing as property so defined seems unquestioned. So far as a man has a right or a claim to live he has one to food, and 'consumption necessitates appropriation'.[2] No duty is more incumbent on all who as voters have any voice in legislation than to consider what possessions ought to be secured to men by law so as to approximate their legal to their moral property, to secure them in the possession of those things to which they have a right.

---

[1] Cf. my article in *Law Quarterly*, January 1940.
[2] Locke, *Civil Government*, ii. 25–51.

For 'no regulation is more constant, more radical and severe than that which is involved in property and the police'.[1]

§ 16. We have already indicated some of the claims which would have to be weighed in such a consideration: the claim to equality, the claim to liberty, the claim of desert, the claim of need, the claim to have undertakings kept, the claim to happiness, the claim to improvement. Our principal attention here will be due to the first two, equality and liberty, for it has been often contended that regulation with a view to the former is incompatible with the latter.[2] My own opinion is that general (that is to say equal) liberty and an equality of possessions would approximately coincide, though of course they might conflict with other claims.

§ 17. Consider the extreme case of unequal possession, where one man had the monopoly of something necessary to all, say of water-supply upon an island. It would also be an extreme case of unfreedom, for all the other inhabitants might be prevented by actual barriers or by fear of death from satisfying their most pressing want. The owner, with adequate police protection, could either let them die or exact any service in exchange for water; they would in fact be enslaved to him merely by inequality of possessions. No doubt if he were a sane human being he would stand drinks,[3] but an institution is not justified by being one which nobody can live down to. Just in proportion as the possession of water were equalized the prohibition of water-theft would become less oppressive even though nobody had as much as he wanted; it would be less obstructive of what each desired to do; the only one who had less liberty would be the original monopolist, and his loss of liberty would not be so great as the gain of even any one of his neighbours, since he could

[1] L. Dickinson, *Justice and Liberty*.
[2] But cf. Croce, 'Libertà e Giustizia' (*Discorsi di varia filosofia*, xvii), and see footnote to § 18, below.
[3] *Non prohibere aqua profluenti.*

hardly have desired to use his superfluity of water, say in cultivating orchids, so passionately as the other desired to moisten his tongue. To be forcibly expropriated from super-abundance or even from convenience impairs liberty less than to be forbidden under penalty to appropriate necessaries. Monopoly of any necessary thing such as house-room may remove all liberty.

If, then, we consider the laws and institutions of property merely as they affect liberty, we must conclude that those are most favourable to it which produce equality in propor-tion to need. Against such equality there may of course be other claims.

§ 18. Those who think that liberty and equality are in-compatible[1] have probably assumed that institutions of their own time and country with regard to property and inheri-tance are eternally founded in the nature of things and are no limitation to the freedom of those who suffer by them. They only consider liberty of action within that legal frame-work, and any reframing which would secure a greater equality of liberty and thereby a greater amount to a greater number they condemn as oppressive. Within the sacred system *laissez-faire* is divinely guided to maximum liberty, but if we do not enforce just that system providence will lead us to servitude.

But that inequalities of possession should be unregulated and that the right of bequest should be unlimited was not generally the belief of the ancients and has not always been recognized in modern states. And such regulation has been defended not only as favourable to liberty or to natural rights but on purely utilitarian grounds.[2]

What, then, are the conflicting claims to possessions which

[1] e.g. Acton, *Lectures on Liberty*; Lecky, *Democracy and Liberty*, i. 212–15; Bagehot, *The English Constitution*; Erskine May, *Democracy in Europe*, ii. 333; De Tocqueville, *L'Ancien Régime*.

[2] M. Arnold, 'Equality' (in *Mixed Essays*): 'On the one side inequality harms by pampering, on the other by vulgarising and depressing.'

might sometimes override the claims to equality and to liberty? Those which are valid can, I think, all be reduced to desert and to general utility, since allowance for need is only in order to secure real equality. A man who has worked has earned or deserved by that very fact more than the man who has been idle when he had the opportunity to work; he has a claim which cannot be reduced to the claim for equality and may conflict with and override it.[1] If, moreover, he can be induced by rewards to satisfy some need of others, they may have a claim either on the ground of equality or on the ground of general beneficence that he should be so rewarded. His own claim, I think, is only to have a bargain kept. The claim put forward to greater possessions or to other advantages on the ground of greater capacity can be reduced, I think, to a claim of others that a man's capacity to increase general happiness or improvement should be realized. The claim to profit by mere displays of talent or by chance discoveries or inventions which are useful but involved no labour, if there are any such, is also reducible to utility.

§ 19. The purely lucky find, as when the schoolboy says 'Bags I, I saw it first', seems nothing more than a device, like tossing up, to avoid quarrels where nobody has any claim. The law does not always recognize property in the finder of treasure-trove.

The claim founded on a long possession which never had any of the grounds already mentioned seems to have nothing in its favour except that a man suffers more by losing what he is accustomed to than by not acquiring novelties, and against this might be set the consideration that it is now somebody else's turn.

I have never felt sure whether the emphatic justification

[1] Locke, *Essay on Civil Government*. Whatever a man by his labour makes out of a natural product is his 'where there is as much and as good left for others'. 'As much as any man can make use of to any advantage of life before it spoils so much he may by labour fix a property in; whatever is beyond this is more than his share.'

of possession on the ground of 'prescription' really means
that what a man has got into his hands, no matter how,
gradually becomes his right by the flux of time;[1] or whether
it is a rather cynical recognition that people are readier to
put up with injustice of long standing than with an act of
unexpected justice which confiscates old and ill-gotten gains,
so that the path of least resistance is to let sleeping wrongs
lie.[2] Of course, if what is meant is that legal recognition of
possessions gives a man legal right and consequently some
moral claim to them, this has been allowed already. If long
possession in itself gave a claim, I think it would always be
overridden by any of the claims I have admitted. Perhaps
the new version of *Beati possidentes*, that what a man now
possesses he must in obscure antiquity have deserved, is the
homage paid by conservatism to virtue.

§ 20. It remains to ask how far property, or the right to
possessions, is transferable or heritable. Men and women
not only may but ought to provide for the nurture and education of their children who may survive them, so far as
these services are not provided by the state. Children, with
whom so long as they are infants there can be no question of
desert, have a claim to equal opportunities of life, happiness,
improvement, and freedom, which implies a claim to the
power of using things, which is a property-claim. If these
claims would not be satisfied in any other way there is an
obligation on the parents to satisfy them, and, in such
circumstances, a legal right of bequest to strangers, which

---

[1] 'Prescription is the most solid of all titles not only to property, but,
what is to secure that property, to government' (Burke, *Present Discontents*). It is 'part of the Law of Nature' (*French Revolution*; cf. *To R.
Burke*). This might seem to justify slavery. Burke applies the same
doctrine to religion (*To W. Smith*).

[2] Hume, *Essays*, I. iv, says: 'Antiquity always begets the opinion of
right', but somewhat inconsistently with his general doctrine he con-
demns this opinion as 'not reason' (II. xvi). Paine remarks that Burke has
'a contemptible opinion of mankind—a herd of beings that must be
governed by fraud'.

contravenes this obligation, is difficult to defend. On the other hand, if the grounds of any claim to possessions have been rightly enumerated (as claims to equality of liberty and of the means to improvement and happiness, claims in respect of desert, and general claims that generally useful capacities should be developed) it is difficult to see that a child with no special merits or capacities has any claim to inherit from its parents what will raise it above the level of equality. It could, of course, be suggested that the power to make such a bequest to one's children or to other persons is much coveted and is an incentive to industry which is generally useful, and that the general claim to increase happiness may override all claims to equality.

Even if we think that a man has a claim to transfer in his life or after death rights of property which he has himself earned by his labour, this is a claim which might easily be overridden by the claims of other persons to equal liberty and opportunities of happiness or improvement, and to the fruits of their own labours, so long as there is not 'so much and so good left for all' or so long as they can make better use of the property 'to any advantage of life'.[1] Titles, lucrative posts, and pensions are supposed to be the rewards of merit, but it is never regarded as unjust that no titles should be bequeathed and some not inherited, nor that posts and pensions should terminate with the first holder.

---

[1] Locke, *Essay on Civil Government*, v. 27–31. On the 9th of February 1946, the Tuan Muda (heir to the throne) of Sarawak had a letter in *The Times* complaining that the Rajah had no right to cede the sovereignty without his consent (as well as that of the people).

INTERNATIONAL RELATIONS

§ 1. I HAVE maintained that our duties to our state do not differ in kind but only in complexity from most of our other duties to our neighbours. Who, then, is my neighbour? The answer seems to be: Any man whose experience I can affect. Our obligations to our fellow countrymen are probably more numerous and often stronger than those to foreigners: more numerous because we have more points of contact, stronger because, among other reasons, we have greater chances of affecting them with less dissipation of energy. I say '*probably* more numerous and stronger'; we certainly often think so. But every vote cast is as likely to affect foreign as domestic policy, and I only think I have a stronger obligation to serve the power, prosperity, justice of my own community, that is of its members, so far as I think these on the whole more conducive to world-wide prosperity and justice than the power and prosperity of other nations.

The moral relations between nation-states and the world are somewhat analogous to those between the family and the nation, with the important difference that to-day the concentration of organized power is on the side of the wider unit in the conflict between family and national loyalty, of the narrower in that between the nation-state and mankind. But this difference has not always held; it was brought about through the replacement of the feudal and clannish systems by the monarchical. We have to hope that similar causes— the improvement of communications, the decline of local autarky, and the resulting chaos between relatively small sovereignties—are now tending towards a similar result. Hobbes's nasty picture of the brutish state of nature, however untrue historically of individual men, has been owned a lively picture of the present relations of states, *imperium imperio lupus,* when peace is a name of the preparation for war; and his baseless story of the foundation of states by contract might turn out prophetically true of an international Leviathan.[1]

§ 2. It has been already said[2] that the ground of our usual obligation not to resist the government, even when we think its laws inexpedient or to some degree unjust, is that almost any effective system of law and order is better than the sheer violence of civil war. The fatal mistake of Hobbes here was, as Locke pointed out,[3] to omit the word 'almost'. If this is the ground of our obligation to obey our state, it would, as Locke also saw, be likewise the ground of an obligation to form or to join one for any rational being who might find himself stateless. And it seems no less the ground of an obligation to work for a super-state or federation of the world in which no nation shall be judge in its own cause. We are often tempted to think with Hobbes that *any* such coercive imponent of law and order would be better than the arbitrament of total war; but we must remember Locke's caution: as civil rebellion might sometimes be a duty to-day, so might world rebellion be under a world Leviathan. But in truth *almost* any rule would be juster and more felicific than war. Yet all government is fiduciary, and there is no guarantee against malversation of trust; we can only try to remove the temptations.[4]

§ 3. It is not the business of philosophy to draw up, even in outline, the constitution of such an oecumenical sovereign; our duty in that business would be opportunist, depending upon the circumstances of the moment, men's general beliefs about them, and their readiness to accept and to implement one or another form. In the abstract, I think, for the reasons

[1] Cf. Kant, *Perpetual Peace* (Supplement I) and *Universal History from a Cosmopolitan Point of View*; Hobbes, *Leviathan*, ii. 13.

[2] Ch. XIV.

[3] *Essay on Civil Government*, §§ 93, 94.

[4] Cf. Plato's denial of private property to his ruling class.

given above,[1] that the ultimate aim should be a democratic representation, and apart from acceptability there seems no reason why states of unequal population should be equally represented. Indeed the block voting of separate states, representing only the majority of each, would not contribute to any impartial consideration for questions of secession by oppressed minorities, vexing questions which seem peculiarly appropriate to international arbitration. Block family voting might not be the best way to get fair treatment for Cinderellas.

I conclude that it is our duty to work for the establishment and continuance of a power able and likely to enforce approximately impartial settlement of disputes in place of the appeal to force, very much as it is our duty to submit our private quarrels to the courts, fallible though they be, rather than to the duel. Such an impartial power would obviously have to be no mere defender of the *status quo*; it would be competent to judge when a demand for the alteration of that state was just and felicific; it must be legislative as well as judicial. Only so could it hope for 'an opinion of right', the moral approval of disinterested parties, on which must ultimately depend that power to enforce its decisions which is one element in its claim to our allegiance, though not, as Hobbes thought, the only element. It must be on the whole just.

[1] Ch. XIV, ii.

PART III

XVII

MORALS AND AESTHETICS[1]

§ 1. I HAVE now tried to follow out the way in which the lines
of moral thinking, as it develops in most men, must work
when applied to political thinking, with, of course, the
conservative, liberal, or revolutionary bias of application
inevitable from our personal history and temperament. It
remains, as I suggested,[2] to trace the relation of the moral
experience with the aesthetic, which has been sometimes
identified and often compared with it, but which is a fundamentally distinct human activity.

I have said[3] that the identification or analogy of morals
with aesthetics seems to me to have been disastrous for both;
it has led to subjectivism in the former and to esoteric
intolerance in the latter. I am not now speaking of the
crudely didactic theory prevailing in the seventeenth century,
by which, as Sidney says, 'the poet . . . doth intende the
winning of the mind from wickednesse to vertue: even as the
childe is often brought to take most wholsom things, by
hiding them in such other as have a pleasant tast.'[4] I am
thinking of a more far-reaching doctrine which maintains
either that goodness and beauty are identical or that, at least,
we apprehend both by a faculty of 'taste' or sense.

§ 2. In Plato there is rather an unconscious assumption of
identity than a deliberate comparison. He used the epithet
καλός without misgiving of νόμοι (meaning just and beneficent
laws, which we ought to enact), of ψυχαί and ἐπιτηδεύματα

---

[1] Parts of this chapter are reproduced, with the Editor's consent, from
my article in *Philosophy*, April 1938.

[2] Ch. XIV.

[3] Ch. III, §§ 1, 2.

[4] *An Apologie for* (*The Defence of*) *Poetrie*.

(meaning just, brave, and temperate conduct and character, not those which are dramatic or arresting), and also of pottery and animal bodies. And he explicitly maintained that beauty, if not identical with moral goodness, is what conduces to it. No doubt he thought both beauty and goodness were real qualities independent of human feelings about them, but the confusion of the two was probably connected in Greek as in modern thought with the accompanying failure to distinguish clearly the fact of obligation from feelings of attraction or repugnance. At the renaissance of moral and aesthetic reflection in this country in the eighteenth century, the identification of beauty either with moral goodness or with moral edification became a commonplace: aestheticians perhaps thinking thereby to recommend their subject to the puritan, and moralists theirs to the polite. The arts were often criticized merely by a didactic standard, and obligation was reduced to mere sensibility. Since most people find a certain satisfaction in contemplating a so-called moral action and a so-called virtuous character, it was overlooked both that they also get aesthetic satisfaction in contemplating the very opposite, and also that the very nature of a moral act is to be done from a belief that we are obliged to it. The question is whether that belief can be true.

§ 3. A moral judgement (e.g. that I ought to pay this money) means something and can be significantly contradicted. But it is not contradicted by denying that I or the majority of people take any pleasure in contemplating the payment. The creditor's claim cannot vary with sympathies, or debts could be cancelled by propaganda and moral verdicts verified by questionnaires. The judgement 'he acted morally' no doubt generally *implies* a feeling of approbation, but it *states* that he did what he did because he believed it his duty; and this belief was not about feelings but about obligation.

It is by no means so clear that judgements like 'The Alps are beautiful' or 'Pope's *Odyssey* is less beautiful than that of

Voss' truly assert any real quality of things other than their relation to human feelings. It is not clear that the Alps always had a quality of beauty though everybody had so far loathed the horrid sight, nor that the second statement could be consistent with asserting that everybody who knew both preferred Pope. And whatever our decision on the point may be, it is a significant fact that what by reflection becomes clearer about the moral judgements becomes less clear about the aesthetic.

It has been long recognized that an object beautiful to my naked eye may seem ugly under the microscope, and that the colours, shadows, sounds, and scents, which play so large a part in aesthetic experience, must be very different to beings with different organs, and can hardly be said to exist as such when they are not being experienced. More recently we have come to believe that even the configuration and movement of what we call physical bodies are very different from anything that we ever perceive. It may be replied that, though people are mistaken in attributing beauty, as they do, to physical things, yet it can be truthfully attributed to sensible appearances,[1] which may be beautiful though nobody observes it. But there still remains to notice a much more interesting characteristic of beauty, suggested already by the Alps and Homer. The beauty of sights and sounds depends, at least very largely, on their 'meaning' for us, and this meaning is different for different persons; in fact, 'it is not they but we who mean'. So 'what I hear' may not only be different from 'what you said', but may affect me differently according as I more or less know the language and your personal idiom and according to the associations I myself have with the words used and the things mentioned, or according to my mood. And if I should hear exactly similar sounds twice, but, owing to such differences, think them

---

[1] Or to 'some more complex whole'. It is hard to discuss this suggestion till it is made more explicit. It may mean just what I do.

beautiful once but not again, it is hard to say at which time, if either, I should be wrong.

This is pretty obvious in literature; hardly less so in painting and sculpture, since the artist seldom denies himself all reference to natural objects, which affect us differently according to our sex, age, colour, climate, training, and religion; and it is not really doubtful about a great part of music and architecture. Sir Donald Tovey, on Beethoven's *Mass in D*, says that in the *Dona Nobis Pacem* 'trumpets and drums are heard with martial rhythm'. This can hardly help affecting one way or another the beauty which a hearer ascribes to the music; yet it must depend on what he happens to know and feel about warfare.[1] At any rate, different systems of harmony are conventional or customary.

Something of the same sort must be true of much natural beauty, and not that only of human face or form. The reason of the almost universal distaste for mountains in the seventeenth century and the almost universal admiration for them in the nineteenth must have been that men had different associations with them or went to them in a different spirit. Ruskin[2] has described with eloquent candour the change in his aesthetic experience of the same visible scene when he discovered that it was not a mist-wreathed Alp but a glass roof behind blue smoke.

Not only may the same sound or vision be beautiful to a man and not to another, or to himself in a different mood, but it may also have entirely different beauties, depending upon his mental habit or condition.

> Thou'll break my heart, thou bonny bird,
>   That sings upon the bough;
> Thou minds me o' the happy days
>   When my fause luve was true.

---

[1] Not that the greatest music and architecture generally convey their 'meaning' by imitating natural sounds or shapes. As Plato and Schopenhauer recognized, they directly express mental states.

[2] *Mod. Painters*, IV. x, § 8.

Not only must this have much more beauty to a reader whose own sorrow has been set to bird-song, but the bird-song itself must have had a very different beauty to Burns, or to the girl he speaks for, when love was false and when it was true.

§ 4. No doubt our attitudes to nature and to works of art, especially to recent ones by known artists, are different. To admire mountains is equally legitimate whether they are thought of as awful solitudes or as happy playgrounds, though the 'beauties' so seen must be different. But, it will be said, an artist *meant* to express something, and we have an historical interest in knowing what it was, as well as a well-founded suspicion that so we shall get the best aesthetic experience out of his work. Yet we do not trouble whether the 'beauties' we find in a ruined cloister or a primitive ballad were intended by their makers or even were found there by their first admirers. That is not a purely aesthetic interest.

Kant[1] tried to exclude all such elements in beauty, which depend upon some conception or meaning or association, from pure or free beauty, and called them dependent beauty. Pure beauty is exemplified only in arabesques, figures, and inorganic objects whose contemplation pleases us by their mere form, such as ripples and perhaps clouds and flowers abstracted from all the sensuous charm of colour and from any thought of adaptation to purpose or of resemblance to other things. It has been questioned, by the Empathy school and by Croce, whether even 'springing' arches or 'gay' colours do not get their beauty from our natural or acquired tendency to read into them some significance, some correspondence with our own activities and affections. But, however that may be, Kant, though rejecting any such hypothesis, cannot allow that beauty is an objective quality of external phenomena or their relations. It is merely the pleasant feeling aroused in us

[1] *Critique of Judgment*, § 16.

by the consciousness of a harmonious free play or our perceptive faculties in apprehending the object:

'The judgment of taste is not scientific but aesthetic, by which I mean that it is a judgment for which the ground can only be subjective. . . . All our ideas can refer to objects, except those only which refer to the feelings of pleasure and pain. Here nothing is indicated in the object, but we have a feeling of ourselves as we are affected by the idea' (§ 1).

I quote Kant as one who, having tried to eliminate from beauty proper all its more obviously subjective elements, all secondary qualities, and all associations or conceptions of use or resemblance, was naturally averse from any expressionist theory. Yet, though he believed that we claim agreement from all men in our judgements about this pure beauty, he was convinced that 'Beauty apart from relation to our feeling is itself nothing'[1]

Even if the simple perception of form apart from any significance were the sufficient stimulus for a genuine aesthetic experience, I should still agree with Richard Price:[2]

'It seems impossible to conceive objects themselves to be endowed with more than a particular order of parts, and with powers, or an affinity to our perceptive faculties, thence arising; and if we call this beauty, then it is an absolute, inherent quality of certain objects; and equally existent whether any mind discerns it or not. But, surely, order and regularity are, more properly, the causes of beauty than beauty itself.'

It must indeed be allowed, as the Provost of Oriel[3] points out, that we commonly *mean* by 'beauty' (as we do by 'pleasant', though not by 'strange') a quality belonging to an object apart from relation to minds; but I agree with him and Mr. Ayer[4] that, on reflection, we see that the things called beautiful

[1] § 9.   [2] *Review of the Principal Questions in Morals.*
[3] Ross, *The Right and the Good*, p. 128 n.
[4] *Language, Truth and Logic*, p. 161. Cf. Rashdall, *The Theory of Good and Evil*, I. vi, note.

or pleasant may not have any common character (as 'surprising' things have not) except the power to produce in some persons a particular kind of experience. 'The actual occurrence of the enjoyment depends on conditions in the experient as well as conditions in the object.' So if one man calls the object beautiful and another calls it ugly, both are wrong if they are asserting it has either independent quality; both may be right if they only mean that it is capable of exciting genuine aesthetic enjoyment and repulsion in different persons.

§ 5. This view is not inconsistent with Kant's claim that we *demand*, though we do not find, universal agreement with our aesthetic judgements—if only the object could, as it never can, have precisely the same emotional significance to all men. Nor is it inconsistent with the distinction of good and bad taste. Bad taste is the incapacity or narrowly limited capacity for pure aesthetic experiences. A man who enjoys contemplating nothing which does not soothe or profit or edify him, or gratify his pride or malice or appetites and affections, has bad taste. He may use the word 'beautiful', but he has few or no aesthetic experiences. The more capacity a man has for pure aesthetic experiences the better his taste, whatever the objects which arouse them. So, too, the more capacity a man has for pure affection, affection that is unmixed with interest or snobbery, the more virtuous he is in that way. In this sphere, unlike the aesthetic, if he is blind to the object's defects no question even arises; but I find it hard to say that, for instance, a mother's love for the son she knows good for nothing is anything but admirable.[1]

Similarly a man is more *moral* (as distinct from being naturally virtuous on the one hand and correctly behaved on

---

[1] Cf. Mme Pasquier and her son Ferdinand in *Le Notaire du Havre*, xv, by G. Duhamel, p. 176. Jane Austen is rather shocking: '[Mrs. Musgrove] had the ill fortune of a very troublesome, hopeless son, and the good fortune to lose him before he reached his twentieth year' (*Persuasion*, vi).

the other) the more moral experiences he has; that is to say, the more acts he does because he believes them to be his duty. The character of what he does in no way affects his morality. There are no effects morally praiseworthy or censurable in themselves apart from the agent's beliefs about his obligations. It is perhaps this analogy between morality and good taste which has contributed to the confusion of moral and aesthetic judgements. But the vital difference for which I have been contending remains. Moral judgements are of two kinds: 'That act was done because the agent thought it his duty and is therefore good,' and 'A given situation involves an obligation on rational beings to act in a certain way and gives other rational beings a claim that such acts should be done.' Both types of judgement seem to be true or false whatever people may think or feel about the acts in question. At least none of the arguments which we have been considering, as tending to show that what is called beauty is a subjective state, seem to apply to obligations. Obligations are not secondary qualities, not indeed qualities of things at all. They arise out of the relations of persons, and there is nothing of whose reality we are more certain than persons. Kant, indeed, held that obligations or, as he oddly called them, the moral law, are the one kind of facts about which, and on the ground of which, we could make synthetic judgements *a priori* that could be true not only of what he calls phenomenal reality but of things in themselves. Nor is Price less emphatic in his condemnation of the 'moral sense school'.

One man may have the pure moral experience in robbing the rich Peter to feed the starving Paul, and another in like situation might have it in resisting the temptation. And this difference may be due, like tastes in scenery, to their environment or upbringing. But once really convince them that they have no real or objective duties to their neighbours and they could have no moral experience at all. On the other hand, Coleridge does not seem from his *Ode to Dejection* to have valued aesthetic experience less for being convinced that beauty lives in seeming.

§ 6. But certain objections, which might be suggested by the last paragraph, require to be met, and I believe can be met, by a more careful distinction. I do not feel these objections to be serious for my main point, but no doubt they have contributed to make plausible the view that obligation is a misnomer for peculiar feelings of pleasure in contemplating certain acts and characters. To begin with, obligations are in one sense mind-dependent in that they would not exist if there were no minds. They are not physical things, nor the relations of physical things or of animals to one another, if our idea of animal consciousness is correct. They arise out of the relations of persons to one another or to other sentient beings. Secondly, there is also a sense in which they depend upon feelings, or rather presuppose that the beings in question have feelings and desires. As Hume pointed out, if all sentient creatures were secure of satisfaction for all their desires, or if they had no desires at all, at least most of our more obvious duties would disappear. I do not see, for instance, how it would be possible to owe anybody anything. At any rate, *what* we ought to do for people must largely depend upon their feelings and wants, and these will to some extent depend upon their beliefs. But since in fact there are sentient beings, some of whom are rational persons, in various relations to one another, and with various desires, the obligations which arise out of these relations are facts whatever anybody may feel or think about them. There is nothing here analogous to the doubt if beauty does not depend on thoughts and feelings. None of these considerations seem to me to make it at all plausible that, when we speak of an obligation to do something, all that is true is that we or others have a particular feeling about acts of the kind. Nor can I think of any other arguments directed to that end.

§ 7. Hume's analysis of moral judgements as judgements about feelings, with his consequent analogy between the moral and aesthetic experiences, was inspired, like modern positivists, by metaphysical and epistemological presuppositions. Both he and they were committed to the doctrine that all knowledge and belief, other than the 'tautological' or analytic connexion of ideas, are derived from sense-experience internal or external; that reason produces no new ideas, can apprehend no necessary connexions, and can supply no ground for action. Consequently he holds that 'goodness' and 'obligation' are merely misleading terms for feelings which we have in contemplating certain acts or characters, and depend entirely upon our temperaments. They are not facts which every rational being would be capable of apprehending. I have criticized these doctrines already.[1]

Next to Hume perhaps the ablest advocate for identifying morality with feeling was Hutcheson.[2] He, however, seems to have allowed a separate 'moral sense', as much distinct from all other pleasurable feelings as sight from smell, though not acting through any special organ. Like Hume he accepted the empirical theory of knowledge without question, but his aim in applying it to morals was quite different. He desired above all to vindicate the intrinsic goodness of benevolence, to show that it was not approved as a means of gratifying self-love, and that consequently our approval of it was immediate and indemonstrable. These characteristics, he argued, are common also to beauty, which is not useful but loved for its own sake, and can neither be measured nor demonstrated. He was precluded from allowing that obligations or goodness could be rationally apprehended as self-evident both by the tradition that reason's only function is reasoning—that it apprehends no truths except analytical judgements and logical implications—and also by the fact that moral self-evidence

[1] Ch. III, §§ 1–4.
[2] *An Enquiry into the Original of our Ideas of Beauty and Virtue.*

seems to differ from scientific self-evidence in arousing emotion and in being a possible ground for action.

Many of the alleged resemblances between moral and aesthetic judgements are real, but they are common to other judgements also. Most moral judgements depend upon capacities for feeling in ourselves or our neighbours, but so do many others; they give rise to feeling, but so do others; they are often influenced by our feelings due to temperament, environment, and history, but so are many scientific judgements. A judgement with all these relations to feeling, yet plainly about a matter of fact, might be 'X is in love with me' or 'The siren has sounded'. It is not only moral judgements which claim immediate hypothetical self-evidence. We can say, 'If this action is possible for me and would increase happiness or goodness I have some obligation to do it', but we can also say, 'If influenza alone invariably follows the assimilation of a certain microbe it is causally connected with it.' Moreover, prior to reflection men often fail to distinguish moral truths from natural or conventional tastes,[1] but also scientific truths from conventional beliefs.

If, then, what Hutcheson means is that the 'moral sense' is essentially different from all other feelings in giving, under proper conditions, certainty of self-evident truth about something not experienced by means of any sense-organ, that is merely a verbal eccentricity. His opponents would be more than justified in replying that moral reason differs from other uses of reason in *necessarily* presupposing feelings and arousing feelings and in being of itself a sufficient ground for action. The point which is not verbal is that moral judgements claim to be true and to have authority over all feelings. Feeling is incorrigible except by habituation, but moral judgements are corrected by thought. If this much be agreed, it might be allowed to describe them with Bishop Butler's irony as 'either sentiments of the understanding or

[1] See Ch. II, § 3.

perceptions of the heart or, which seems the truth, as in-cluding both', and to leave greater precision as 'a useful occupation for persons of leisure'. Here, perhaps, Butler is making a concession to Hutcheson whose utilitarianism he seems in the same *Dissertation*[1] to be refuting; but it is not inconsistent with his earlier criticism of Shaftesbury.[2]

§ 8. My conclusion is that our moral and aesthetic judge-ments differ fundamentally in this: It is at least very ques-tionable if, on reflection, we can believe that things have what we call beauty whether anybody is affected aesthetically by them or not. All that may be true is that some or all things are capable, under certain conditions, of affecting persons in that way, as they may also be capable of affecting them with surprise or pleasure. And if this were true, we should have no less reason to enjoy our aesthetic experiences or to distinguish them from other pleasant experiences or to value them in proportion to their vividness and purity. On the other hand, reflection on our moral judgements more and more convinces me that the relations in which we stand to our fellows are in objective fact grounds of real obligation. And if we could really cease to believe this, and be persuaded that when something is called our duty all that is true is that some people have certain feelings about it, the moral ex-perience would become impossible for us. If we really sometimes are under obligations, there is goodness in acting from the belief that we are so on a given occasion; if not, not. And it seems to me undeniable that there is. But the goodness of aesthetic experience does not depend upon beauty being a quality of objects.

---

[1] *On the Nature of Virtue.*   [2] Quoted above, Ch. III, § 1.

DATE DUE

MAY 23 '89			
NO 9 '90			
NO1 3 '99			

DEMCO 38-297